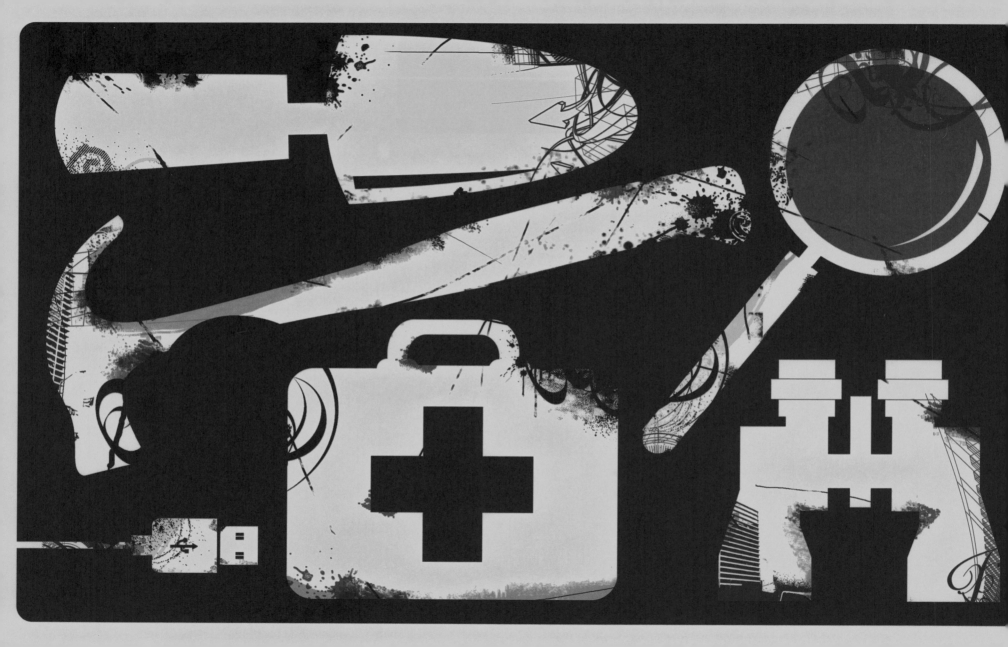

IT'S MY LIFE!

A GUIDE TO ALTERNATIVES AFTER HIGH SCHOOL

Edited by Janine Schwab

**American Friends
Service Committee**

ACKNOWLEDGEMENTS

We express our deep appreciation to American Friends Service Committee's (AFSC) Orita Program and NC Choices for Youth for allowing us to use their book *What's Next? A Guide For North Carolina Teens Wondering What's After High School* as a foundation for this national guide. We are grateful to the author Pam Schwingl, the editors Marnie Clark and Curt Torell, and Orita Program Director Ann Lennon for their inspiring work.

We also thank Devon Davidson, Karen Cromley, Hallie Kelly, Rebecca Farabaugh, and Mary Day Kent for their writing and editing contributions, Dorothy Lazenbury-Gibbs for assistance with production and distribution, and Tony Heriza and AFSC's Office of Educational Outreach, without whom this book could not have been produced.

Book design by Design for Social Impact, www.dfsi.org

The descriptions in this book are derived from websites and other sources provided by the included organizations and programs. All details are subject to change. We strongly recommend that you visit the organizational websites for the latest information.

ISBN: 978-0-91008-251-8

American Friends Service Committee
It's My Life!
1501 Cherry Street
Philadelphia, PA 19102
Ph: 215-241-7176
Web: www.afsc.org/itsmylife
Email: itsmylife@afsc.org

TABLE OF CONTENTS

INTRODUCTION

You're wondering what to do after high school. You are not alone. Many young people are not sure they want to go to college right away. Others don't have the money. You may want to learn something new. You may want to help other people.

DO YOU WANT TO:

Have an adventure?

Work to save the environment?

Work with animals?

Learn new skills?

Serve your country?

Try out a career?

Earn money for college?

This guide lists training opportunities, internships, and apprenticeships.

YOU WILL:

Learn to solve community problems.

Put your beliefs into action.

Make new friends.

You'll become more aware of what you value, what's important to you in a job, and what you really want from life. You also can save money for college.

You may feel pressure to decide now—but you do not have to make any decisions quickly that you might regret later.

Remember! You do not have to decide RIGHT NOW what you want to do with your whole life!

HOW TO USE THIS BOOKLET

"It's My Life!" contains ideas to get you started in your own decision making process. A state or local guide may also be available online with local contact information and resources for many of the options discussed in this booklet. Please visit **www.afsc.org/itsmylife** or call 215.241.7176 to find out.

INSIDE "IT'S MY LIFE!"

"It's My Life!" has information on:

• Finding money for education and training.

• How to survive the transition from high school to the real world—especially if you're not planning on college right now.

"It's My Life!" has articles on:

• How to think about what you might want to do now and in the future.

• How to get more information on careers, and

• Some very cool ways you can serve your country and make money for college at the same time.

Some of these opportunities are open to people without a high school diploma or who have not passed the General Educational Development (GED) test. Joining many of these programs does not mean a long-term commitment.

This information is meant to help you get started. Once you begin exploring all the possibilities, you will find even more options beyond the ones listed here.

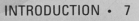

"It's the start of your life...
Go for it"

1:

SURVIVING THE
NEXT FEW YEARS

Are you almost out of high school? Have you been out for awhile but still not figured out what to do with your life? You're not sure what's next, but you know you're in for some changes— a temporary job, different school, even taking a year or two off from college or a career to explore. You may even be thinking about the military. Whatever you're thinking about doing, each choice means a choice NOT to do something else. So, it's a good idea to get a big picture of the options you have before making any decisions.

This section has some information on what it feels like to make a change, what you might consider doing in a year off, and how you can start thinking "out of the box."

For starters, make the Internet your friend. They don't call it the "World Wide Web" for nothing—it is literally your access to millions of ideas and options. We've got some tips on how to find Internet access near you.

Some of your plans may include finding your own place to live, so we've included a Basics Training Guide for finding shelter, meals, and transportation as well.

When you're making changes—from high school or something else—not knowing can be the hardest part.

TAKE SMALL STEPS IN EXPLORING

Make smaller changes instead of a huge leap that you may not be ready for.

What's Exciting to You?

• What inspires you to get involved?

• What are you passionate about?

• What makes you feel alert—energized mentally, emotionally, and physically?

• What are you doing when you lose track of time?

• When you're talking with the most excitement, what are you talking about?

• What ideas, images, or people keep showing up in your life?

Experiment

- Test reality by taking action (take a class, apply for a job). Try out your ideas.

- Take the risk of going down different roads and learning from DEAD ENDS. They'll be there. Don't worry about that. Follow any road that intrigues you.

Find people who support your personal choices and connect with people who:

- believe in you

- provide healthy support

- provide constructive criticism

- NOT people who are negative or don't provide support for your important choices

Make Yourself and Your Health a Priority

Bad habits can make you less alert, cloud your thinking, and limit your ability to engage fully in your life.

- Pay attention to what you eat. Eat less sugar and more protein, fruits and vegetables and drink lots of water.

- Get enough sleep. Not getting enough sleep can make you depressed.

- Be active and physical. Even a short walk helps.

- Limit time with people and things that distract you from what you really want to do.

Explore Your Options

- This is the time to get information and explore your options.

- The best choices may come to you in stages. Trust that it will all make sense eventually.

- Don't try to sort it all out now.

- LIVE FOR AWHILE WITH THE QUESTIONS and enjoy thinking about the excitement of the future.

Remember! It's OK to NOT KNOW what to do next.

TAKING A YEAR OFF

You may not be quite ready to decide what's next. Many people who see no immediate interesting prospects after high school feel scared and pressured.

Maybe you can't go to college for one reason or another, or you just don't feel like being in school again.

So what will you do?

You don't have much money. Your parents and teachers are pressuring you to make a decision, and those recruiters and camouflaged hummers are looking increasingly cool.

Sometimes, though, it works better to take a year off to work, travel, do something really weird, make some money for college, or just breathe deeply before launching into the next thing. School and the military will always be there, waiting in the wings. Don't jump before you are ready.

Many different programs have sprung up to help youth recently out of high school make the best use of this "time off." This year off is also known as a "gap year."

Some of these gap year programs are pricey and out of reach, especially if you're already struggling financially. But many other options are quite possible.

Look at the offerings below — and page through the rest of this guide — to get ideas about how to spend some time learning something different and having a little adventure at the same time. **Working during your year off can give you an opportunity to raise some cash, as well as give you time to think about what you really want to do with your life. And the skills you learn and experiences you have can be useful later on.**

Gap-Year Information Sources

WhereYouHeaded? is a subscription-based service that helps young people plan time off after high school or time off from college by maintaining a database of opportunities and advice on anything from scheduling and budgets to college applications. A six month membership is $80 and a full year membership is $120. Any student who qualifies for an SAT fee waiver is entitled to a free membership at the site. Of course, you don't need to pay money to access all kinds of information and opportunities. But if you like a little more structure and help, see **www.whereyouheaded.com**

Jobs and Service

- **Teens4Hire.org** is a membership-based website founded in 2002 and dedicated to linking teens with prospective employers. Students may take a career assessment test, read about labor laws and work permits, and search for jobs. **www.Teens4Hire.org**

- **Public Allies** selects individuals ages 18 to 30 for a 10-month program of leadership training, team service, and paid, professional internships in community nonprofit organizations (Ally Leadership Program). Ally positions are funded by AmeriCorps and include a monthly stipend of about $1,500, health insurance, childcare, interest-free student loan deferment, and a post-service education award of $4,725. **www.publicallies.org** or call 414-273-0533

- **AmeriCorps** (see articles in Section "National Service" on AmeriCorps*NCCC, AmeriCorps*Habitat, and City Year). **www.AmeriCorps.org**

PUBLIC ALLIES TEAM SERVICE PROJECT:

Teams of Allies collaborate to design and implement projects that benefit the community. Examples of past projects include creating a video about alternatives to jail, helping residents create a community garden, and facilitating teen leadership programs.

• **The Dynamy Internship Year Program** offers internships and independent living in Dynamy apartments along with an Outward Bound program, one-on-one advising, and optional college credit seminars for 17 to 22 year-olds. Dynamy, Inc. is a not-for-profit experiential educational organization, the oldest residential internship program in the country. Its mission, as stated on its website, is to offer young people, ages 17 to 22, a gap year opportunity like no other. Dynamy programs integrate independent city apartment living with mentored internships, personal and college/ career advising, urban and wilderness leadership opportunities, and the company of other young people.

Locations: Worcester, Massachusetts and Santa Rosa, California. It is expensive. It costs $17,000 a year, plus $7,000 for room and board. There are lower-cost, half-year programs available and some financial aid.
www.dynamy.org

WEBSITES TO VISIT

www.whereyouheaded.com
A site that offers interesting educational options, helps people make plans to take a year off, and offers advice for the college application process. There is a fee but it can be waived if you are low-income.

www.Gap-year.co.uk
This is a British site, but it has a lot of good ideas about the gap year, including information about staying safe and healthy.

www.yearoutgroup.org
Another British site with information on gap years for students, advisors and parents.

www.youthtravel.org
A new website with information on how to travel safely.

www.unitedplanet.org and www.gquest.org
These sites offer travel abroad service and educational opportunities.

www.interimprograms.com
The Center for INTERIM Programs asks: If you could wave a magic wand, what would you do?

Outdoor Experience

• **The Outward Bound Wilderness** website claims that it is the nation's leading, non-profit adventure-education organization offering an array of exhilarating course activities in many of the beautiful and pristine wilderness areas throughout the United States and internationally. The courses emphasize personal growth through hands-on experience and challenges. Students of all ages develop self-reliance, responsibility, teamwork, confidence and compassion, as well as environmental and community stewardship. It is expensive but may be worth saving up for if you really want to learn about the outdoors. **www.outwardboundwilderness.org**

BOOKS TO CHECK OUT

The Gap-Year Advantage, by Karl Haigler and Rae Nelson (St. Martin's Griffin; 2005)

One of the few books for U.S. students interested in a gap year, this book has ideas for a gap year after high school and taking time off while in college.

The Back Door Guide to Short-Term Job Adventures: Internships, Summer Jobs, Seasonal Work, Volunteer Vacations, and Transitions Abroad by Michael Landes (Ten Speed Press; 4th edition 2005)

Or ask a librarian!

THE
CIRCUS?

Photo courtesy of Airplay Trapeze School, www.airplaytrapeze.com

Joe, approaching the end of high school in Durham, North Carolina, decided to join the circus—that's right—the circus! He had learned how to juggle in school. What started as a crazy fun thing to do for a while after high school became a six-year stint working in a family circus and traveling the country.

Joe learned skills he never knew about and had time to think about his values, interests and goals. He decided he wanted to be an artist and had saved enough money, so he applied to a design school where he is currently studying.

If you want to learn more about going to school to become a circus performer, visit **www.americanyouthcircus.org** for a list of training programs.

Remember!

You have choices, you can take some time, and you don't have to feel pressured to leap into something you're not sure about.

Dog sledding? Elephants? Shoeing horses? Guitar Building? Take a look at some examples of real job opportunities that might whet your appetite for adventure! While many of the options may not really be something you would want to do, they show that fun, interesting, unconventional jobs exist. Use your imagination and think about what you would really like to do and then find it!

NATURE'S KENNEL SLED DOG RACING

Nature's Kennel Sled Dog Racing is a professional sled dog racing kennel that also provides dog mushing and winter camping adventure vacations. Nature's Kennel is home to 60 sled dogs, located in the remote wilderness of Michigan's Upper Peninsula.

Job Description: What you will be doing: A LOT! EVERYTHING! You name it, you might do it. Your main task will be getting the yearlings and adult teams ready to race and do everything that goes along with racing.

Qualifications: How often do we need you? 24/7! This opportunity requires somebody who can stay active seven days a week, all day long (sometimes all night as well) and maintain a positive attitude.

Salary Benefits: You will receive $150/month for food and a place to sleep. You will also get an opportunity to run our yearling team in the annual Iditarod or run our yearling team in the U.P. 200 and Can AM Crown. All race expenses will be covered.

Availability: Must be available for entire program (a $300 tip is given if you stay until the end).

Contact: Nature's Kennel at 906-748-0513 or **www.natureskennel.com** to see if they are still accepting interns.

HORSE SHOEING TRAINING PROGRAMS

If you love horses and the outdoors, learning to shoe horses can be a well-paying profession, or can supplement a less lucrative one!

Proper education is the best way to start. Schools and training programs offer various levels of study ranging from short two-week courses to intensive yearlong programs. Most cost something, but farriers ("horseshoers") can make up to $150 per hour for their services.

If you're interested in becoming a skilled farrier, start with this website: **www.horseshoes.com/schools** for links to horseshoeing schools all over the globe.

GUITAR BUILDING

There are many options available to those interested in studying luthiery—guitar making.

There are many schools offering courses in guitar building across the country and throughout the world. The website **www.buildyourguitar.com/ resources/schools.htm** is a great place to start looking for guitar building schools both in the U.S. and abroad. The website **www.cybozone.com/fg/become.html** lists additional schools, as well as apprenticeship opportunities.

Additionally, **www.luth.org/schools.htm** offers information about online courses.

BOAT BUILDING

Learn to build boats, develop carpentry skills, become an accomplished sailor, and perform community service—all as an apprentice at the Carpenter's Boat Shop in Pemaquid, Maine.

The Boat Shop experience has no cost; nor do you earn money in the apprenticeship, though you are free after normal work hours to work at another job. The real payoff for the apprenticeship is the experience, both in work and in the community life.

During the year you will learn:

• **Boatbuilding:** how to loft, frame, and construct traditional Maine sailing and rowing craft.

• **Safety:** how to care for, use properly, and maintain carpentry tools, machinery, and equipment.

• **Carpentry:** how to build basic pieces of furniture including a tool box, Shaker oval boxes, and a small writing desk.

• **Seamanship:** how to row safely and sail the various craft the Boat Shop builds.

• **Resourcefulness:** how to make do with limited materials.

The Carpenter's Boat Shop is located in Pemaquid, Maine. It operates out of two farmhouses on twenty-one acres of land near the Pemaquid River. Apprenticeships are for a period of nine months, from September until mid-June. Apprentices must be 18 years or older.

The life of the Boat Shop is supported by the sale of boats built by apprentices and by the generous gifts of individuals.

Visit **www.carpentersboatshop.com** for more information.

THE ELEPHANT SANCTUARY

The Elephant Sanctuary accepts applications for six-week internships. The intern positions are not paid positions. Housing is provided but interns are responsible for their own food and transportation.

Job Description: Interns work five days per week and are required to work weekends. Interns assist the head keeper in all aspects of daily care, cleaning, and feeding.

Qualifications: Interns are chosen for their field of study, experience, and future goals. Internships are awarded to students studying veterinary science, zoology, wildlife management, and related fields, as well as to those drawn to the Sanctuary for spiritual reasons.

If you are interested in applying send your resume, availability, and three letters of recommendation to kate@elephants.com

SHELTER

One of the first and most important things you'll need to do when you set out on your own is to find a place to live. Short-term? Long-term? Roommates? Solo? Location? Transportation? There are a lot of things to think about—some practical, some personal.

Some Tips:

• The more roommates you have, the cheaper everything will be.

• Most landlords will require a deposit at the beginning of your lease, and it's usually at least one month's rent.

• Most leases last for one year. Some places have shorter or month-to-month leases. If you sign a lease, it's going to cost a lot of money if you want to leave before it's up, so be sure you want to stay put before you sign a long-term lease. You may also need a co-signer if you're under 21.

• Keep in mind the cost of utilities.

• Some landlords and apartment complexes include some utilities in the rent. Ask about this since it reduces your expenses.

Free Housing?!

There are a number of ways to find free housing, including entering a program where housing is provided. On your own, options include: becoming a live-in nanny or babysitter or bartering housekeeping or landscaping work for a free room in someone's house.

Housesitting

For housesitting opportunities, see **www.caretaker.org** and **www.housecarers.com**.

Temporary Shelter

Youth hostels: In many larger cities and most states, you will find youth hostels that are safe, clean and provide temporary shelter. If you are adventurous enough to travel, check out this website, **www.hihostels.com**, to find out which states have hostels and what facilities they have. Hostel prices range from $10 per night in smaller cities to $29 in New York City. Travelers Aid helps those who are stranded. See **www.travelersaid.org**.

Emergency or Safe Shelters

A Safe Place is a community program that sets up public locations as a network of places where youth in crisis can get immediate help. The YMCA has a hotline number and safe places you can go if you find yourself needing temporary shelter. Call 800-621-4000 to find out where one is near you.

A GOOD DEAL

Tim was young, unemployed, far from his hometown of Boston, and lacking a high school diploma. After a series of dead-end jobs and losing his apartment, he placed an ad on Craigslist (**www.craigslist.org**) to barter building skills for a free housing situation. He found a family who needed some remodeling done which didn't take up much of his time. He found he had time to think about the next steps in his life and get his GED. He still wasn't ready for college, though. Instead, he planned a trip by bicycle with his best friend across the country from the East Coast to Oregon and even wrote to a few bike manufacturers to sponsor his trip. One of them agreed!

If you don't have a bike, some communities have earn-a-bike programs, where you can learn to fix up a bike you earn through community service. For information, see **www.bikecollectives.org**, or **www.ibike.org**.

BEYOND SHELTER

Need a Shower? If you're not looking for a shelter, but just a place to shower and get coffee and breakfast, there may be community centers and other places in your area that offer such services.

Need a Meal? There are places to go for a meal in most communities across the country.

For access to immediate resources, see **www.nationalhomeless.org/resources/ state/index.html**. You will find a list of organizations that may be able to help direct you. Otherwise, try the library, Salvation Army or YMCA, or a church, mosque, or synagogue for help.

Both federal and state governments offer benefits that may help you gain access to affordable housing, meals, and possibly even health care.

www.govbenefits.gov is a website that asks you a series of questions about your income, age, family status, and other factors to determine which state and federal benefits you might qualify for.

NEED A WAY TO GET TO WORK OR SCHOOL?

Ride boards, "Smart Commute," and other ride-sharing programs have become more popular along with the soaring price of gas. Every day hundreds of thousands of people drive the route you take between your house and your job or school.

If you don't have a car, you may be able to contribute money for gas to someone who does. If you have a car, you can share the price of gas, or carpool—in other words, you can take turns driving with someone and both save money.

You can also use the Internet to get in touch with people from your area looking to carpool. **www.erideshare.com** is a free service connecting people throughout the country to carpools in their community. **www.craigslist.org** is another source of ride share information.

IF YOU NEED EMERGENCY HELP

The National Drug Abuse Hotline can help you find a local treatment program if you think you might have a problem with drugs. — 800-662-4357

CDC Info Hotline provides referrals to local health testing sites and information on health care topics such as HIV/AIDS and other sexually transmitted diseases. — 800-CDC-INFO

The National Runaway Hotline works with runaway youth and their families, either helping youth (to age 21) get home with free bus tickets, or just helping them find a warm bed. — 800-621-4000

National Suicide Prevention Lifeline helps those at risk for suicide and those who are worried about a friend or family member committing suicide. They also have a Myspace page at www.myspace.com/suicideprevention-lifeline. — 800-273-TALK

The GI Rights Hotline helps youth in the military sort out their options if they are having second thoughts about military life. — 877-447-4487

HOW TO FIND A PLACE TO RENT

- **ohmyapt.apartmentratings.com** This site offers tips for helping you find an apartment, important questions to ask potential landlords, and a list of organizations that deal with renters' rights and laws by state under "Renters' Resources."

- Read the Classified ads in newspapers.

- Look for 'For Rent' signs from the street.

- Use local lists such as **www.craigslist.org**.

- Check out bulletin boards at local businesses, schools, and community centers. College bulletin boards and newspapers are an especially good source for youth-friendly housing.

Almost all libraries have computers with Internet access.

Most have some rules about how long you can stay online. Some, but not all, may require a library card, so it's a good idea to phone before you make a trip. If you're not sure how to get started, ask the Librarian— she or he can give you tips about using the Internet.

You may also be able to access the Internet at public terminals in community and youth centers or for a fee at an Internet café. Also, try your local job or career center or rec center.

LIBRARY
SCOOP

Libraries are unique places to find information on jobs and educational opportunities. At a library you can do a lot more than browse listings. Where else can you look up a word you see in a help wanted ad that you're not sure of, or find books on any subject related to the career you are researching? Librarians are used to answering questions from jobseekers and many libraries have special rooms or areas specifically devoted to job hunting. Some hold special lectures or seminars on topics such as resume writing and successful interviewing.

At a library, you can:

• Read more about careers in books and magazines

• Think about continuing your education in a trade school or at college

• Prepare for tests required for a job or to get into school

• Make lists of potential employers

• Write resumes and cover letters

• Learn about community organizations that help with training or job placement

• Read books about people who do a job you find interesting

Just ask, the Internet is your key to the future!

"PUSH!

try something really hard."

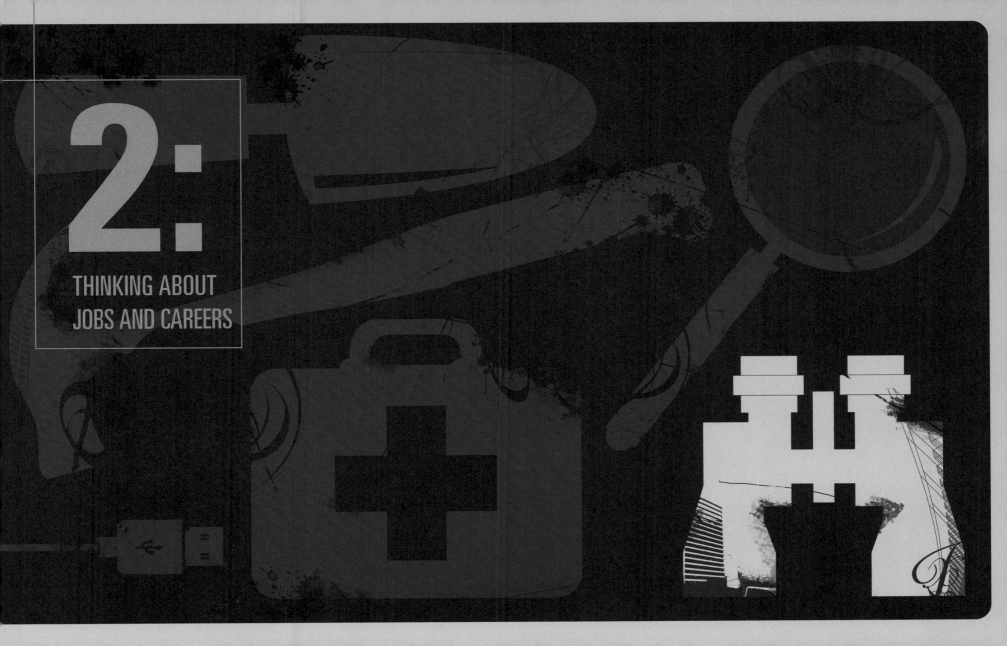

2:

THINKING ABOUT
JOBS AND CAREERS

Do you ever fantasize about what you'll be doing to support yourself when you're older?

Or does it just give you a headache to think that far ahead?

Are you worried that your next decision has to be the "right one" for the rest of your life?

What makes you tick? What do you really like to do?

This section will introduce you to some ideas to take the mystery out of thinking about your future!

NEXT STEPS

The important thing now is to stay open to new ideas, search out new information, and keep "trying on" different ideas or jobs to see what brings out the best in you and what fits best with your deeper values.

Don't worry that you are wasting time trying out different jobs. You will pick up skills and interests in any job you take. Learning to work with other people is one skill that is useful in any job.

Of course, you can also read about different occupations, online or at the library. You can talk to people about what they like and don't like about their jobs.

Training

If you feel like you want to get more training before you make a leap, you can take courses on any subject that appeals to you. And you don't need to pay for expensive classes to get a taste of many careers. Community colleges, universities and nonprofit organizations often offer courses on a wide range of subjects to the general public.

Ask the Experts

You can set up a formal internship where you work in a field that interests you. If you are not ready for that kind of commitment, you can request what is known as an "informational interview". This may sound very formal, but all it involves is setting up a time to talk to someone who does the job you are interested in and visiting them at their workplace.

Most working people are happy to help a young person. They will be flattered that you are interested in what they do.

Hot Jobs

We've included a list of "hot jobs" later in this chapter. These are jobs that experts have predicted will have a lot of openings in the next few years. But don't decide what to do just based on what other people say will be a hot job. The situation may change. Listening to your gut and following your interests may end up leading you to something the experts could not have even predicted would be a "hot job".

A REALLY
HOT JOB

Glassblowing is an example of a career with many entry points. Glassblowers blow hot melted sand into bottles, sculpture, lampshades, and industrial and scientific equipment. You can learn how to be a glassblower by:

• Apprenticing at a master blower's shop

• Entering a formal apprentice program at a company

• Taking weekend classes at an art studio

• Entering a formal training program at a community college or vocational school

• Majoring in art at a liberal arts college or university

Each of these choices involves a different level of financial and time commitment. You might end up sequencing your choices, starting out with an informal "hobby" class, moving on to a school program or apprenticeship later, and, finally, doing additional on the job training. You don't need to jump into an expensive program or school right away to explore most careers!

Find a Hobby

What do you do in your spare time? If you have a hobby, you might become skilled enough in it to make it your career. Even singers who never get famous still find jobs teaching music or directing choirs. You might also benefit from some entrepreneur classes on how to start your own business (see page 68 for ideas). If you have the motivation to become an "expert" at something, you might just have the energy to start your own business doing it. One woman we know turned her skills writing music and playing the saxophone into a business where she did musical presentations in schools and for community groups.

Find a Counselor

Talk to a career counselor, but don't expect to get all the answers from them. Counselors can help you with resources and advice, but without you taking into account your values and expectations, their advice may not be very helpful.

The good news is counselors can help you with identifying your values and skills by recommending some assessment tools (see page 29 for some tests you can do yourself). These tools can help you identify your own strengths and interests, so that you can decide which career path will work best for you.

Photo courtesy of Philadelphia Weekly

WARNING: A JOB YOU CAN'T QUIT!

It's true most of the time that you can just change jobs or quit, but there is one major exception. If you decide to join the military, leaving may be impossible without breaking military law and going to jail. It is also difficult to switch jobs in the military – the military does not want to waste their investment so, if you train as a cook, don't expect to be able to switch to computer tech later.

Skills and certifications you earn in the military may have no civilian counterpart once you leave. We know a man who trained to refuel military jets only to be told he would have to start at the bottom and retrain when he applied at the airlines after he was discharged. Some occupations, like human resources, have such different rules, that there is little application in the real world.

If you decide to join and then change your mind, the GI Rights Hotline can help you explore legal ways to get out. Their phone number is 877-447-4487. **For more information, see www.girightshotline.org.**

The most important part of choosing a career is to focus your own interests, values, goals, and skills.

Do you like to help other people? Would you like to serve your community? Want a flexible work schedule? Like outdoor work? Want as much leisure time as possible? Do you thrive on working closely with other people? Or do you like working alone and independently? Is prestige, security, or a high salary most important to you?

Several free tools are online or at most job counselors' offices that can help you learn about yourself and what kind of job you might enjoy.

These "self-assessment tools" can be an important step in your journey of self-discovery and thinking about what you want to do.

Basically, self-assessment tools help you understand your values, interests, personality or skills. Some tests help you figure out your likes and dislikes.

Other tests help you understand your personality. A personality inventory looks at your individual traits: what drives you, what strong needs you have, and your attitudes. The most frequently used personality inventory is the Myers-Briggs Type Indicator (MBTI). **www.myersbriggs.org**

ASSESSMENT TOOLS

An assessment tool is like a test. But you are not graded like in school. The results help you understand your values and skills. They are often fun and interesting to take. There is no pass or fail!

You may have already taken a test at school called the ASVAB or participated in the Career Exploration Program. The ASVAB (Armed Services Vocational Aptitude Battery) is actually the military's entrance exam, but many schools use it to test for civilian careers. The ASVAB test is designed to detect aptitude for military jobs, however. If you want to know about other jobs, you should take a civilian test.

Other tools assess your learning style. Several are listed at **www.ulc.arizona.edu/assessments.htm**.

For a great selection of fun tools, go to **www.queendom.com**.

Many resources can be found at **www.jobhuntersbible.com/counseling**

Having or getting skills isn't the end of your search. Where will you use them? To what end?

For example, computer skills are helpful in many jobs and necessary in some. But if you're skilled with computers, don't grab just any computer job. The content of the work should fit with your values and goals as well.

That's work satisfaction—contributing to something you believe is worthwhile.

Computer work for a firm that is doing work you don't approve of—like causing pollution or cheating people—would leave you dissatisfied, however skillfully you performed the job.

Some college graduates take the "Graduation Pledge of Social and Environmental Responsibility" when they get their diploma. It states, "I pledge to explore and take into account the social and environmental consequences of any job I consider and will try to improve these aspects of any organizations for which I work."

Students define for themselves what it means to be socially and environmentally responsible. **You don't have to wait for a college degree, though, to pledge to making the world a better place.**

For ideas, check out **www.idealist.org**, an online job search site for connecting social change organizations to potential employees.

USEFUL GUIDES

Useful Guides To Self Discovery

Here are some great books you might want to check out. Try the library or go to a bookstore.

The Career Guide for Creative and Unconventional People, by Carol Eikleberry (Ten Speed Press; 2007) **www.creativecareers.com**

Discover What You're Best At: The National Career Aptitude System and Career Directory, by Linda Gale (Fireside; 1998)

The Best Work of Your Life, by Patricia V. Alea and Patty Mullins (Perigee Trade; 1998)

What Color Is Your Parachute? For Teens, by Richard Nelson Bolles (Ten Speed Press; 2006)

"I pledge to explore and take into account the social and environmental consequences of any job I consider and will try to improve these aspects of any organizations for which I work."

IDEAS FOR FINDING A JOB OR PLANNING A CAREER

TAKING THE MYSTERY OUT OF WHAT'S NEXT

"What's Next?" seems like a simple enough question, but answering it can be a complex process.

The perfect job for you may be one you haven't yet heard of; the career path you think is too hard or costly may actually be within reach; the job you thought you wanted may not be a good fit at all.

Exploring options is an important first step down any path. If you need help, you'll find resources below for learning about jobs and careers.

Remember, people working in the jobs you might want will most likely be happy to talk to you. Some may be able to suggest ways to get started with an internship or training.

IN-PERSON HELP

It's best to talk with people who are "in the know"—school counselors, people at job fairs, ministers, parents, or friends of parents.

You can also go to career websites online, but there's no substitute for talking with professional job counselors.

ONLINE HELP

Many websites have information useful for exploring job opportunities and training programs.

Some provide general information and guidance; others list specific job openings. Browse!

Career and Tech School Finder:

One good site is **www.khake.com**. On this site you can explore vocational and technical careers, check out the skills employers really want, find a trade school, research technical topics, and take a look at the current job market.

You can find any community college in any state on this site: **www.aacc.nche.edu**

Career Info:

To find out about wages and employment trends, occupational requirements, state-by-state labor market conditions, employer contacts nationwide, financial aid information, and the most extensive career resource library online, visit America's Career InfoNet website: **www.acinet.org**

OTHER HELP

Check out:

300 Best Jobs Without a Four-Year Degree, by Michael Farr. (JIST Works; 2005).

This is a great book for people who want to make the most of their training and those who want to explore new career options without going back to school.

INTERNET RESOURCES

Job Search Websites

www.idealist.org (also includes paid and unpaid internships and volunteer opportunities)

www.indeed.com

www.craigslist.org

www.careerbuilder.com

www.monster.com

www.hotjobs.yahoo.com

www.teens4hire.org

JOB SHADOW

A good idea, in this economic climate, is to "job shadow" (go with an adult friend to his or her job, ask questions, watch what that person does, or look for an internship or apprentice opportunity). Start to learn what people do in different jobs. Once you see actual possibilities, you'll have a better idea of what you'll want to do. There are choices; you'll just have to look around to see them!

The numbers of openings in these jobs is expected to grow the fastest during the next five to seven years. Fastest Growing Occupations, 2004–14 (Bureau of Labor Statistics, 2005)

1. Medical Assistants

2. Network Systems & Data Communications Analysts

3. Physician Assistants

4. Social and Human Service Assistants

5. Home Health Aides

6. Medical Records & Health Information Technicians

7. Physical Therapist Aides

8. Computer Software Engineers, Applications

9. Computer Software Engineers, Systems Software

10. Physical Therapist Assistants

11. Fitness Trainers and Aerobics Instructors

12. Database Administrators

13. Veterinary Technologists and Technicians

14. Dental Hygienists

15. Hazardous Materials Removal Workers

16. Irradiated-Fuel Handlers

17. Dental Assistants

18. Personal and Home Care Aides

19. Self-Enrichment Education Teachers

20. Computer Systems Analysts

21. Occupational Therapist Assistants

22. Environmental Engineers

23. Teachers, Postsecondary

24. Computer Security Specialists

25. Network and Computer Systems Administrators

THE ECONOMY: WHAT DOES IT HAVE TO DO WITH YOU?

Most of the new jobs today are in service industries – businesses that don't manufacture items, but sell products or services, like a clothing store or a travel agency.

Many U.S. workers are finding there are more and more jobs in the retail sector, i.e. "McJobs". Landing a job that pays a good salary usually means getting specialized training and skills. Pay attention to your career path early on, so you will be able to land jobs that can support you.

FOR MORE INFORMATION ABOUT CAREERS

See the federal government's Occupational Outlook Handbook at **www.bls.gov/oco/home.htm**. For hundreds of different types of jobs—such as teacher, lawyer, and nurse—the Occupational Outlook Handbook tells you:

- the training and education needed
- earnings
- expected job prospects
- what workers do on the job
- working conditions

At **www.careervoyages.gov**, you can explore different careers and even watch videos about what they are like!

AN IMPORTANT REMINDER

Remember: "Hot" jobs may or may not be a good choice for you. And today's "hot" jobs may not be plentiful a few years from now.

Learn about yourself first and explore the jobs that fit you!

"The best things are done for OTHERS"

3:

SERVING YOUR COUNTRY

Do you see yourself being a hero for your country? If so, you can become one in many ways.

One way is to become a member of AmeriCorps. This is a civilian organization that provides many opportunities to serve while you are learning skills and earning money for college. In the wake of Hurricanes Katrina, Wilma, and others, AmeriCorps joined with local, state, and federal relief and recovery efforts to provide emergency assistance and long-term relief. AmeriCorps also partners with smaller nonprofits and agencies that provide all kinds of services in communities all across the country. For more information about benefits and the history of the program, see **www.americorps.org**.

If you want to have the experience of living with a group of young people who are also looking to do something for their country, AmeriCorps* NCCC (National Civilian Conservation Corps) may be the best choice. You will live dormitory style and be deployed to areas of the country where work is needed on projects that help communities. **www.americorps.gov/about/ programs/nccc.asp (see next page)**

For the more independent minded, AmeriCorps* Habitat sends team members to live in communities to build housing. AmeriCorps* Habitat does not provide housing but they help people find housing while they build. For more information, see **www.habitat.org/cncs (see page 40).**

If you would like to work with children, City Year, the program that inspired the creation of AmeriCorps and a member of AmeriCorps, might be right for you. The website is located at: **www.cityyear.org (see page 41)**.

There are literally thousands more AmeriCorps options, some of them probably right where you live! **Many nonprofits have at least one or two AmeriCorps paid service opportunities, so don't restrict your search to just the biggest AmeriCorps programs.** The benefits are the same whether you are tutoring kids in the city or building hiking trails in the wilderness, so take the time to find if there is a program that will really utilize your interests and talents. Ask local organizations that you like if they have an AmeriCorps slot, or take the time to search at **www.cns.gov**.

You can also call AmeriCorps at 800-942-2677 or write them an email at questions@americorps.org.

Note: A GED or high school diploma is not required for many AmeriCorps service opportunities.

Careers that promote peace and justice are numerous, too; we've listed some ways for you to find out more about how to get involved with organizations working for change. And of course, being a hero is possible throughout your career if you choose to work in any of eighty different types of health care jobs that play a role in preventing and treating illness.

AMERICORPS*NCCC:

SERVING YOUR COUNTRY AWAY FROM HOME

If service is one of your goals, the AmeriCorps*National Civilian Conservation Corps (NCCC) may be just the right choice. It allows you to serve your country, live away from home, and do so as a civilian.

The NCCC arm of AmeriCorps is somewhat like our domestic Peace Corps. Its mission is to strengthen communities and develop leaders through national and community service.

You will serve for 10 months and live in a dormitory with a group of other young people. Food and health care are provided, along with travel to and from the program. There is a $4,000 stipend plus an educational award worth $4,725. Money for child care is available for parents in the program. The age limit is 18-24.

Team members must be able and willing to perform physical labor, sometimes in stressful environments and adverse weather conditions. And they must be willing to serve long hours beyond the eight-hour workday, deploy to any location in the region served by the campus, and deal with sudden and unexpected changes.

CONTACT INFORMATION

AmeriCorps*National Civilian Community Corps (NCCC)

Principal program sponsor: AmeriCorps

Phone: 800-731-0002

www.americorps.gov/about/ programs/nccc.asp

There are many opportunities to serve while you are learning skills and earning money for college.

AMERICORPS HABITAT

You may have already heard of Habitat for Humanity, but may not have known that Habitat, usually a volunteer organization, hires 18 to 24 year old AmeriCorps workers to help build housing for Habitat families.

Habitat for Humanity builds and renovates sturdy homes for low-income families who provide a good part of the "sweat equity" themselves.

Habitat is a Christian-based organization, but is open to anyone, regardless of his or her faith. **www.habitat.org**

You will receive safety and construction training and you'll be given a chance to develop skills as a community leader and construction supervisor.

Habitat pays for travel and helps you find housing. There is a $10,600/year stipend and a $4,725 educational award at the end of service. Child care and health insurance are available.

Habitat is based in Georgia but its projects are all over the U.S.

CONTACT INFORMATION

AmeriCorps*Habitat
121 Habitat Street
Americus, GA 31709

Phone: 800-422-4828, ext. 2293
Fax: 229-924-2096
Email: americorps@hfhi.org
www.habitat.org/cncs

Volunteering with kids can be tough, but it is definitely rewarding.

CITY YEAR

If you are interested in an urban experience and you like the idea of working with children, consider signing up with City Year.

You will serve for 10 months in a major U.S. city. City Year will help you find housing and provide health insurance and transportation. There is a stipend and an educational award of $4,725.

CONTACT INFORMATION

City Year Headquarters
285 Columbus Ave.
Boston, MA 02116

Phone: 617-927-2500
Fax: 617-927-2510
www.cityyear.org

PEACE AND SOCIAL JUSTICE JOBS

Do you want to serve your community and your world? Many jobs are available that build community, reduce barriers between people and create peace and justice. Jobs working for better living conditions, the environment, reduction in warfare and racial justice are all about working for peace!

In most of these jobs, people skills are important. Enthusiasm, showing respect for others, being aware of others' feelings, showing up, being on time, and having patience when things don't go your way will help you succeed.

Most important is your dedication to the cause of doing right in the world or repairing an injustice. Many social justice organizations have internships or volunteer opportunities.

Sometimes, there are paid internships available for young people who have not yet gone to college.

Many organizations working for social change highly value their volunteers and may eventually move a dedicated volunteer into a paid job or make referrals to paid positions.

INTERNET RESOURCES

Spending some time volunteering gives you a chance to see if these are areas you'd like to pursue. You can learn about the field and whether it's a good fit for you, and you can show co-workers and supervisors what you can do. Who knows? A job offer may follow! Try **www.volunteermatch.org** to find volunteer opportunities in your area.

Check out **www.idealist.org** for internship and volunteer opportunities and **www.future5000.com** to connect to other youth in the peace and justice movement. If you are especially interested in youth-led social activism, see **www.freechild.org**. They have a list of youth-led activist organizations.

A FEW EXAMPLES OF CAREERS IN PEACEMAKING AND SOCIAL CHANGE

OCCUPATION	WHAT YOU CAN DO IN THIS JOB	SKILLS NEEDED
ARTIST	Use art to communicate about important political and social issues; provoke people to think about them.	Natural talent; formal art education can help.
COMMUNITY ORGANIZER	Work for a group trying to change conditions in your community. Do something about issues like housing, racism, pollution, poverty, discrimination and war.	Talent for getting things done; ability to work well with others; knowledge of issues.
ECONOMIST	Work to create economic justice for all; study world economics and advise policymakers on how to remove the economic causes for conflict.	Advanced college degree.
HEALTH PROFESSIONAL	Become a paramedic, doctor, massage therapist, a nurse, or other health care worker and bring better medical care to others.	Depending on career: vocational certificate, junior college or advanced college degree.
JOURNALIST/WRITER	Research, uncover and write about local and world problems and bring them to the attention of others; help inspire people to take action.	Writing talent, interviewing skills; college/special training not required but helpful.
LEGAL PROFESSIONAL	Help improve the legal and political system by working to pass better laws. Work for policies that promote peaceful solutions to conflict.	Depending on career: vocational certificate, lower college degree, or advanced law degree.

A FEW MORE EXAMPLES OF CAREERS IN PEACEMAKING AND SOCIAL CHANGE

OCCUPATION	WHAT YOU CAN DO IN THIS JOB	SKILLS NEEDED
LOBBYIST	Help improve the legal and political system by working to pass better laws. Work for policies that promote peaceful solutions to conflict.	Organizing skills, ability to work well with the public, creative mind, knowledge of political system
MEDIATOR	Become a trained mediator and help resolve disputes between and among individuals, families, businesses and labor.	Patience, fairness, positive attitude; vocational training.
POLITICAL CANVASSER	Work as a petition circulator to put issues on the ballot; or go door-to-door as a canvasser for social and environmental groups.	Ability to work with public and communicate clearly; positive attitude helpful.
RECYCLER	Help improve the environment by working for a company that recycles metal, paper, plastics or other products.	Different skills can be useful, depending on the job.
SOLAR INSTALLER	Help reduce our dependency on oil, coal, and nuclear power by working for a solar energy company.	Plumbing, electrical, carpentry skills.
TEACHER	Help improve the educational system; teach the next generation of young people how to improve their lives and the world.	Patience, creative mind, college required for most jobs.
UNION ORGANIZER	Work for better wages, a healthier work place and labor justice.	Organizing skills, strong commitment to representing fellow workers, knowledge of trade or business involved.

Table provided by Project YANO in San Diego, CA. For more ideas about careers in peacemaking, see www.projectyano.org.

CONNECTING WITH AN ORGANIZATION

You can often get your feet wet with a large, national organization that supports local activism with resources like brochures, local chapters, and information about special issues.

Some of these organizations have special youth sections and youth activist trainings and internships. Some even offer paid positions canvassing neighborhoods. All of the following organizations offer ways you can get involved right away.

American Friends Service Committee (AFSC) www.afsc.org — One of the largest and oldest peace and social justice organizations. With programs in most states in the country, AFSC can often use volunteers in its work for peace and conflict resolution, youth empowerment, criminal justice, and immigrant rights.

NAACP (National Association for the Advancement of Colored People) www.naacp.org — The NAACP has one of the largest organized groups of young people of any secular organization in the country.

National Council of La Raza www.nclr.org — La Raza is the largest national Latino advocacy organization in the U.S. and has a special youth section.

Amnesty International www.amnestyusa.org — Amnesty is an international human rights organization, assisting political prisoners and victims of torture and working against the death penalty, in the United States and overseas.

Sierra Club www.sierraclub.org — One of the largest environmental organizations in the country, Sierra Club takes on everything from factory farm practices to clean energy initiatives.

National Organization for Women (NOW) www.now.org — NOW takes positions on all issues that affect women's lives, including racism and economic justice.

The Ruckus Society www.ruckus.org — Ruckus exists to assist other organizations and movements with creating more effective campaigns for change. They offer trainings and action camps.

National Urban League www.nul.org — The Urban League can be found in most urban centers empowering African Americans and working to improve community organization.

ACORN www.acorn.org — ACORN works on all issues that have an impact on low-income Americans, including housing, lack of paid sick leave, racial injustice and lack of health care.

Public Interest Research Group www.uspirg.org — U.S. PIRG has local affiliates in every state working for health care reform, clean air, food safety and for higher education access.

Jobs With Justice www.jwj.org — With offices in most states, Jobs With Justice has national campaigns for worker justice, health care, immigrant rights, and more.

United for Peace and Justice (UFPJ) www.unitedforpeace.org — UFPJ works to end war and promote justice, in the U.S. and overseas. Local actions and groups in all 50 states.

Congress of Racial Equality (CORE) www.core-online.org — CORE does crisis intervention in communities in conflict, as well as crime victim's assistance and immigrants' rights work.

CREATING YOUR OWN CHANGE

Another option is to develop your own program for social change. The website www.freechild.org lists youth activism grants and scholarships that reward youth activism. Every organization and individual struggles with funding. But more and more people see youth as the key to a hopeful future and are willing to bet money on the results of youth activism.

For help getting started, check out the Youth Activism Project (YAP). YAP's goal is to encourage young people to speak up and pursue lasting solutions to problems they care deeply about.

YAP can help you decide how to work on your issue with email and telephone advice through their hotline 1-800-KID-POWER. They give advice on getting legislation passed, working with government officials and how to communicate effectively with older adults on youth issues. They also offer trainings, a newsletter, and books and manuals which teach best practices for making change.

Youth Activism Project, Inc.
P.O. Box E
Kensington MD 20895
Toll-free: 1-800-KID-POWER
Phone: 301-929-8808
Email: info@youthactivismproject.org
www.youthactivismproject.org

ACTIVIST TRAINING

Special training is often available for learning how to work on an issue. Some trainings teach about a specific issue you may be concerned about and others teach general skills for making change. Learning how to communicate your ideas and work with other people to achieve a common goal are learned skills. Many trainings and internships have been created specifically for young activists.

"Everybody can be great...because anybody can serve. You don't have to have a college degree to serve. You don't have to make your subject and verb agree to serve. You only need a heart full of grace. A soul generated by love." Martin Luther King, Jr.

PAID ACTIVIST TRAINING INTERNSHIPS

Center for Third World Organizing

The Movement Activist Apprenticeship Program (MAAP) is an 8-week-long intensive training program that provides people of color with the opportunity to develop skills and experience in grassroots organizing. For the past 20 years, MAAP has been the Movement's flagship organizer-training program for people of color, bringing motivated young activists together from all over the country to teach them the science and art of organizing communities around their most salient issues. MAAP has trained more than 300 organizers, many of whom currently hold positions of responsibility within social-justice organizations around the country. In order to be considered, applicants are required to go through one of CTWO's Community Action Trainings (CAT).

Interns will be full-time staff members of organizations and will be provided with a $250/week stipend (before tax), temporary health insurance, as well as secured housing and local transportation accommodations for the duration of their fieldwork.

CTWO will cover the cost of round-trip travel between Oakland and their placement sites. CTWO determines placement through several considerations: the need of the host organization (i.e. language, gender, particular skills, etc), the organization's geographical location, the general pool of interns and hosts. Although interns may express preferences, CTWO makes final decisions about where interns are placed.

For more information, see **www.ctwo.org**.

Midwest Academy

Founded in 1973 the **Midwest Academy** is a national training institute committed to advancing the struggle for social, economic, and racial justice. From local neighborhood groups to statewide and national organizations, Midwest Academy has trained over twenty-five thousand grassroots activists from hundreds of organizations and coalitions. Midwest Academy teaches an organizing philosophy, methods and skills that enable ordinary people to actively participate in the democratic process. Courses and consulting services are designed for progressive organizations and coalitions that utilize civic engagement activities to build citizen power at all levels of our democracy.

The Midwest Academy, a 33-year-old national training institute for progressive direct action organizing, hires community organizing interns for a paid ten week Summer program. The stipend was $3000 in 2007, and is paid biweekly.

Interns will receive a week of training similar to the Midwest Academy five-day training. They will learn how organizers choose issues, develop strategy, assess their own organizational power, recruit constituents, and move into action. (Costs for the training, including room/board, are covered.)

During the nine weeks in the field, interns will conduct community outreach and organize one or more public meetings. Interns receive day-to-day supervision from their placement organizations, and ongoing training and mentoring from the Midwest Academy. For interns who are interested in pursuing a job in community organizing, Midwest Academy provides job search assistance at the end of the internship or upon college graduation.

For more information, see **www.midwestacademy.com**.

UNPAID ACTIVIST TRAINING INTERNSHIPS

Mexico Summer Project

For close to 70 years, American Friends Service Committee has sent youth to rural Mexico once a summer for the Mexico Summer Project. The trip brings together young people from different countries for seven weeks of intercultural exchange, service work, and reflective learning among the indigenous communities of rural Mexico.

There is a participants' fee, but generous scholarship opportunities are available. After a week of orientation, including a 3-day home stay with a local host family, participants are divided into five groups. Each group of 10 to 14 participants includes two project facilitators. Each diverse team lives as a community; they share chores and cooking responsibilities, and sleep on cots in a room in a school or community building. All activities are conducted in Spanish and Spanish proficiency is required.

Youth teams will spend their mornings on assigned projects for sustainable development and other physical work helpful in the community such as working in the fields, hauling fire wood, repairing walk ways, etc. In the afternoon, participants will engage with local families in cooking, arts, music, language workshops and other interactive, cultural activities.

Project activities are done in collaboration with the Indigenous families. Projects for sustainable development are determined based on community needs. Workshops are enriched by the skills and interests of participants and community members.

Participants should not come to learn Spanish nor to boost their ego by helping those in need. The principal objective is to give and receive in a cultural exchange with others, to learn from local systems of community organization, and to reclaim values of justice, multi-cultural relations, and cooperation.

For more information, visit **www.afsc.org/jobs**

PEACEMAKER TRAINING INSTITUTE

THE FELLOWSHIP OF RECONCILIATION OFFERS PEACEMAKER TRAINING INSTITUTES (PTI'S) FOR YOUNG PEOPLE.

The Peacemaker Training Institute helps young people become more effective peace and justice activists. PTI trainings held across the country offer:

• Nonviolent strategies to deal with interpersonal and systematic violence, racism and other social injustices;

• Opportunities to network with other active youth from diverse cultures;

• Leadership, communication and conflict resolution skills;

• Interaction with experienced activists working for peace, equality and community empowerment;

• Hope and inspiration for the future;

• The confidence and ability to make a difference.

PARTICIPANTS

Trainings are open to all people ages 17-25 including high school and college students, workers, and young people not employed or in school. Young people of color and others who do activism for survival, including GLBTQ, ESL/non-citizens, and working class youth, are encouraged to apply.

COST

The fee for participation in a Basic PTI is $475-$625, on a sliding scale based on ability to pay. Fees for the Advanced PTI and Local PTI can vary. Organizers work hard to ensure that everyone who wants to attend a PTI is able to attend. Organizers offer fundraising support in the form of sponsorship suggestions, local FOR group contacts, other organizational contacts, and help with any necessary documentation. Fees cover program, materials, food, housing and local transportation for the week. Participants must arrange their own transportation to the training site.

LOCAL SPONSORSHIP

Past participants have benefited from sponsorship. University student groups, campus ministry programs, local peace and justice groups, churches and community/ service organizations have all provided financial support to participants in the past, and have been strengthened by the skills and insights contributed by these individuals after completion of the program. Organizations are encouraged to consider sponsoring one or more members to a PTI and/or advanced PTI with an understanding that participants will return to their organization or community to help organize a PTI or other work with young adults.

For an application, contact:
Brie Phillips
Peacemaker Training Institute
Fellowship of Reconciliation (USA)
1050 Selby Avenue
St. Paul, MN 55104

Email: pti@forusa.org
Ph: 651-757-5353
www.forusa.org/programs/pti/

PROMISING CAREERS IN SERVICE TO OTHERS

Health care offers it all: Work that's exciting and on the cutting edge of science and technology; the opportunity to serve others; jobs that pay well and have excellent potential for advancement.

The U.S. Department of Labor reports that seventeen percent of all new jobs between now and 2010 will be in the health care industry. To fill these, 4.2 million workers will be needed.

Why so many jobs? An explosion of new knowledge and technologies for finding and treating disease, a growing elderly population requiring more services, and the rapid growth of alternative and complementary medicine are some of the factors that guarantee a significant growth in the number of these jobs over the next decade.

EDUCATION AND TRAINING REQUIREMENTS

As you might already know, many health care careers require some education past high school. Fortunately, many training programs are available for people interested in health careers. Furthermore, the U.S. educational system offers a number of support programs to prepare students for health career training.

So even if you didn't study much math and science in high school, the health career path is still open to you. Many community college programs offer math and science courses to prepare you better for a health career.

Where to Start?

Here are a few websites you may want to check out if you are interested in getting training for a healthcare career.

• Healthcare Careers' website lists training programs in a wide variety of medical and allied health care fields. The listings include online and distance learning courses. The website also includes a list of career opportunities in allied healthcare. **www.health-care-careers.org**

• All Allied Health Schools' website provides a list of schools throughout the country where you can train for a career in the healthcare industry. **www.allalliedhealthschools.com**

Try Learning for Life's career exploring program and get placed in a health care organization. They also have programs in: Arts & Humanities; Aviation; Business ; Communications; Engineering; Fire Service; Law Enforcement; Law & Government; Science; Skilled Trades; Social Services. www.learningforlife.org

ADDITIONAL INFORMATION

Here are some ways to get more information about health care career opportunities:

• Talk to people working in a health profession. Ask them why they chose this field, what they do, and what they like and don't like about their jobs.

• Volunteer in a nursing home, doctor's office, or hospital.

• Read about health careers on the Internet or ask the reference librarian.

• Read publications in the field that interest you.

• Find out about events you can attend in the community and on local community college and university campuses.

• Take an introductory course in the field in which you're interested.

BEYOND DOCTORS
AND NURSES

Health care jobs aren't just nurses and doctors. There are about eighty different kinds of health care professionals.

These include clinical research monitors or study managers, medical illustrators, phlebotomists, occupational therapists, dental hygienists, nursing assistants, health information technicians, radiation technologists, substance abuse counselors, respiratory care therapists, health care administrators, and many more.

Some medical careers involve protecting the environment and workers from toxic substances—such as occupational health and safety specialists or environmental health specialists who test water and soil or inspect restaurants and swimming pools.

Even if you didn't study much math and science in high school, the health career path is still open to you.

"Travel will open your

EYES AND YOUR MIND"

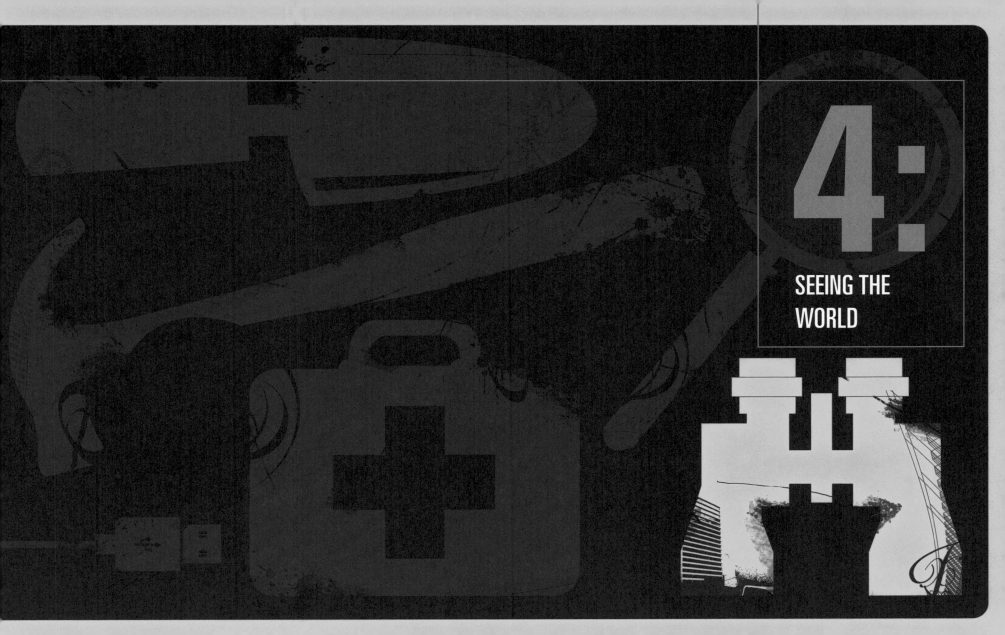

4:

SEEING THE WORLD

Would you like to experience living in another culture? Would you like to visit another country? Or just see what it's like the next state over? Travel can be an important part of your plans over the next few years. You need to be open to new experiences and take some risks with your emotions to get in touch with a different culture. But almost everyone who travels says that it broadened their outlook and changed their life for the better.

WHAT YOU NEED

If you do plan to travel overseas, make sure to apply for your passport very early, at least two months ahead. Passport applications can be found at post offices. You will need to buy special passport-sized photos to hand in with your application, along with $97. You will need identification and proof of citizenship. If you do not have a driver's license, you can get a state ID from the state where you live, which will work just as well.

You will also need money while you travel. One option is to carry traveler's cheques, but this is often not as convenient as carrying a credit card. If you do not have a credit card, most bank cards that operate as a Visa/debit or Mastercard/debit will work really well. Cash machines in foreign countries often work on the same system as in the United States and the money is exchanged for you, as you withdrawal it. You will need to keep in mind the exchange rate, so you can keep track, but, otherwise, it is very simple.

Other than basic clothing and personal items, plus plans for where you will be traveling, you do not need much. Packing light works out much better than packing too much, especially if you are traveling via train, bus, or plane.

GETTING STARTED

Travel can include almost any kind of activity and people travel for all different reasons. Maybe you like to surf and you want to see the big waves in Hawai'i. Or maybe you want to learn a language. Or maybe you want to build peace through cultural exchange and volunteering.

Whether you just want to get away or if you have a special goal for your travels, budgeting for a trip is easier if you stick to low-price airfares and low-cost local transportation. Here are some ideas for traveling on the cheap.

Transportation

To save on plane tickets, you can try using discount air travel sites like www.travelocity.com or www.expedia.com. For the real experts on youth travel, though, turn to STA Travel. They specialize in youth and student fares which can be much cheaper than regular adult fares. They can help you get an International Student Identity Card (ISIC) if you are still in school or an International Youth Travel Card if you are not yet 26 but not in school. Both will entitle you to various youth discounts while traveling. For more information, see www.statravel.com.

If you want to travel to Europe, make sure you look into Eurail passes available for your destination. Traveling around on rail passes can be a cheap way to see a lot of countries. If you combine rail travel with staying at inexpensive youth hostels, you can make a dream trip very cheap. STA Travel (www.statravel.com) sells rail passes. For travel in the United States, you can buy Amtrak rail passes. See www.amtrak.com. Or you can travel by bus on a Discovery Pass www.discovery-pass.com.

Don't forget to budget travel once you get to where you are going. Taking local public transportation instead of taxis is cheap and often a good way to get the lay of the land and see how ordinary people live.

Housing

Youth hostels are designed for youth in that they are inexpensive and promote youth-friendly activities. Each hostel is run differently, however. Some are open all night; some have curfews and if you don't make it back in time, you are on the street for the night. Reading guide books designed for youth travel like the Let's Go series (www.letsgo.com) and the Lonely Planet series (www.lonely-planet.com) will clue you in to what individual hostels are like and list alternatives. For a listing of youth hostels all over the world and information about hostelling, see www.hiusa.org.

If you get stuck with no money, food, or shelter, check if there is a Traveler's Aid office where you are staying (in the U.S., Toronto and Australia). Traveler's Aid helps people who become stranded while traveling due to emergency. **www.travelersaid.org**

INTERNET RESOURCES

www.transitionsabroad.com

Listings of jobs all around the world, plus general travel tips and personal travel stories. Transitions Abroad is actually a magazine that you can subscribe to.

www.coolworks.com

Lists seasonal jobs in unusual and beautiful places like resorts, with a special section just for national parks. You might end up doing the same old boring job as at home, but wouldn't you rather do it somewhere cool?

For ideas on how to work abroad to finance your travel by working, check out: Work Your Way Around the World by Susan Griffith (Vacation Work; 2007)

OPPORTUNITIES LEARNING AND VOLUNTEERING ABROAD

Travel can be about seeing the sights and relaxing, but it can also change your life. If you want to learn and grow while traveling, volunteering or working abroad may make your experience more meaningful. Participating in international workcamps is a good way to experience other cultures and help with some very worthy projects, alongside other international volunteers.

Service Civil International (SCI)

"Peace through deeds, not through words" is SCI's motto. They promote worldwide short term and long term voluntary service to impact social, environmental and humanitarian issues. Through various non-profit partner organizations worldwide and through the SCI network of international and regional development, SCI participates in the exchange of over 5,000 volunteers each year in short term 2-3 week international group workcamps and in long term 3-12 month volunteer postings in over 50 countries.

Participants are young and old, wealthy and not-so-wealthy, and come from all over the world. The only requirement is a commitment to take part in building peace through cross-cultural understanding and hard work. Sometimes there is a fee for participation in the workcamps and sometimes expenses are covered. Travel expenses to the site are always the responsibility of the workcamper.

Main Office:
5505 Walnut Level Road
Crozet, VA 22932
Ph: 206-350-6585
Email: sciinfo@sci-ivs.org
For more information, see
www.sci-ivs.org.

Volunteers for Peace (VFP)

VFP provides intercultural education through community service. They place people in over 3400 projects in more than 100 countries each year, including over 40 in the U.S. At each project, volunteers from diverse backgrounds, typically from four or more countries, work and live together like a family. The sharing of everyday life, both with the local community and among the international volunteers, is an integral part of the learning and serving experience. Most projects are open to volunteers with any type of background and do not require any specific professional or language skills.

Volunteers For Peace
1034 Tiffany Road
Belmont VT 05730
Ph: 802-259-2759
Email: vfp@vfp.org
For more information, see www.vfp.org.

International Cultural Youth Exchange (ICYE)

Through ICYE, young people aged 18 to 25 (up to 30 in certain countries), with or without qualifications, after high school or during college or (un)employment, have the opportunity to live in another country with a family or in a residential project, and work as volunteers in a wide variety of voluntary work placements.

To be a volunteer with ICYE means to integrate in the life and work of the hosting organization and wider community. Volunteers are encouraged and supported to get involved in the planning and managing of distinct activities, take part in staff meetings, and to take on responsibilities according to their skills and interests, as well as the needs of the project. An important aspect of the voluntary service experience is the volunteer's active participation in the life of the community in which he/she lives and works.

In the United States, ICYE is partnered with United Planet (UP). UP is an international, educational, humanitarian, and peace-building, non-profit organization with members and volunteers in over 150 countries devoted to fostering cross-cultural understanding and friendship, supporting communities in dire need, and promoting social & economic prosperity among cultures in order to unite the world in a community beyond borders.

United Planet
11 Arlington Street
Boston, MA 02116
Ph: 617-267-7763
Toll-free: 800-292-2316
Email: quest@unitedplanet.org
For more information, see
www.unitedplanet.org and
www.icye.org.

SERVAS INTERNATIONAL

Do you really want to get to know people in the country you are visiting? Become an individual peacemaker between countries? Membership in Servas International might be for you. Servas members join a database of either hosts or travelers. Hosts welcome international travelers into their homes for up to two nights (more if the arrangement is mutually agreeable). Guests are free to contact any Servas hosts anywhere to try and arrange for a short homestay. **For more information, see www.servas.org.**

"Following your interests leads to SUCCESS"

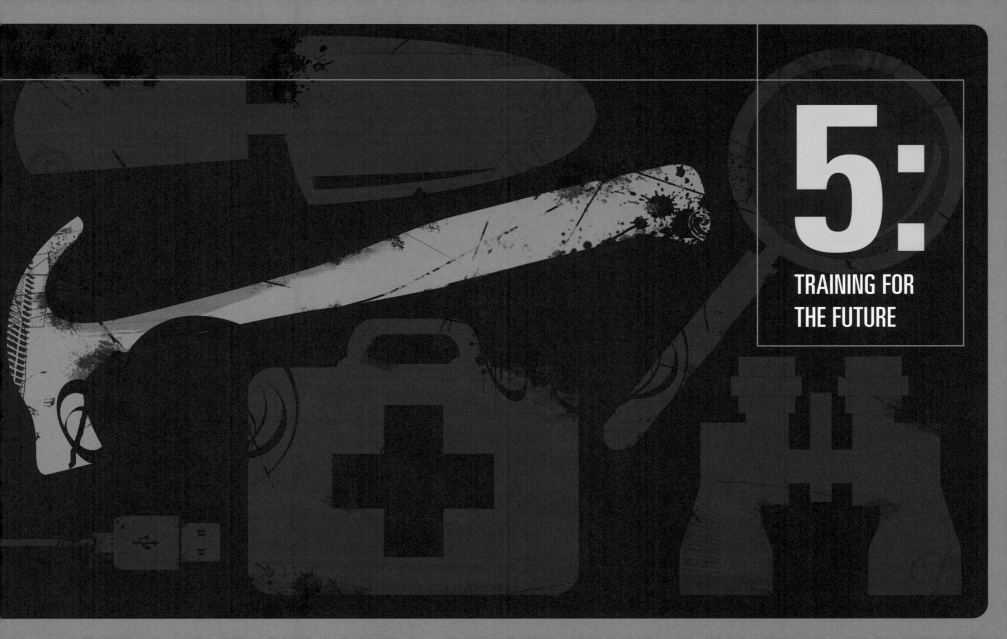

5:

TRAINING FOR THE FUTURE

SKILLS TRAINING AND APPRENTICESHIPS

Here are several ideas about getting skills training—from programs you might find in your own community to those requiring you to relocate. You can "earn while you learn" in an apprenticeship program.

Other programs require a hefty commitment to school for at least a while. Still others require less time in school but promise fairly high wages after completion of the program.

Many skills programs are offered in the community college system across the country. You can find any community college in any state on this site: **www.aacc.nche.edu.**

EARN WHILE YOU LEARN

- **Apprenticeship:** Training in an art, trade or craft under a legal agreement that defines the duration and conditions of the relationship between master and apprentice.

- **Journeyman:** A skilled worker who is qualified by experience and training to undertake the tasks necessary for employment.

GET AGE OLD TRAINING FOR THE 21ST CENTURY

You may have read about apprenticeships in your history books. But these centuries-old, formalized job training programs are rapidly gaining popularity throughout the country. You "earn while you learn" as an apprentice—acquiring valuable vocational skills on the job.

Apprenticeships are available not only in the manufacturing sector but also in service, retail, and government trades. Opportunities in your state are most likely to occur in industries that want more trained employees.

Apprenticeships give employers the opportunity to train you the way they want you to be trained and to see how you do on the job.

Afterwards, companies are likely to hire the people they've trained—workers who have not only learned the skills, but have also demonstrated a good work ethic and dependability.

For the apprentice, these programs provide an income while learning.

You can visit Career Voyages, a government sponsored site that allows you to view videos of different careers. **www.careervoyages.gov/apprenticeship-main.cfm**

Explore Local Companies

You also can call a company or trade union you may be interested in working for to ask if it has a certified apprenticeship program.

CAUTION: Just as with any contractual relationship, make sure you read the fine print in the apprenticeship agreement and know what you're committing to and what you'll receive.

School Partnerships

Many high schools have partnerships with companies that offer apprenticeships. Your school guidance counselor can help you find out if there are such programs at your school.

INFORMATION SOURCES ABOUT APPRENTICESHIPS

U.S. Department of Labor Employment & Training Administration

The Employment and Training Administration provides high quality job training, employment, and labor market information.

The Office of Apprenticeship Training, Employer and Labor Services website (OATELS) provides information on how to begin an apprenticeship and provides links to national apprenticeship programs, as well as programs in your own area that especially focus on young adults. See **www.doleta.gov/OA** and **www.doleta.gov/jobseekers**.

APPRENTICESHIPS

Fields Offering Apprenticeships

Aerospace

Automotive

Biotechnology

Construction

Energy

Financial Services

Health Care

Hospitality

Information Technology

Manufacturing

Retail

Transportation

Concerned About Global Warming? Gas prices? Be part of an alternative fuels program. Did you know that 199 million cars burn 4,000 gallons of gasoline every second in the United States?

If you love cars and want to contribute to the environment and our economy in a big way, think about taking part in an alternative fuels curriculum.

There are National Alternative Fuel Training Consortium (NAFTC) training centers in twenty-four states throughout the Unites States. The goal of NAFTC is to establish a national pool of trained automotive technicians skilled in the operation, maintenance, and safety of Alternative Fuels Vehicles.

More than 5,500 technicians have been trained in hundreds of organizations, including the U.S. Postal Service, the U.S. Air Force, Clean Cities Programs, and commercial fleets.

Course instructor Rich Cregar of West

Virginia University, the headquarters for NAFTC, says the new national curriculum is unique. Classes teach about alternative fuel vehicles, system integration and service of natural gas vehicles, and CNG cylinder inspection and certification of natural gas vehicles. Training is given on propane vehicles, as well as transient emissions.

The course on alternative fuels is the first class NAFTC designed that is intended for anyone interested in alternative fuels and all of the issues—energy independence, ecology, global warming.

Here's a list of training centers located throughout the United States:

Phoenix, Arizona
Whittier, California
North Haven, Connecticut
Lakeland, Florida
Ankeny, Iowa
East Chicago, Indiana
Lafayette, Indiana
Cicero, Illinois
Baton Rouge, Louisiana
Arlington, Massachusetts
Baltimore, Maryland
Kalamazoo, Michigan
Lansing, Michigan
St. Louis, Missouri
Raleigh, North Carolina
Columbus, Nebraska
Las Vegas, Nevada
Syracuse, New York
Cleveland, Ohio
Lima, Ohio
Portland, Oregon
Warwick, Rhode Island
Rock Hill, South Carolina
Nashville, Tennessee
Fort Worth, Texas
Shoreline, Washington
Morgantown, West Virginia

CONTACT INFORMATION

**National Alternative Fuel
Training Consortium (NAFTC)**

Headquarters:
Ridgeview Business Park
1100 Frederick Lane
Morgantown, WV 26508

Ph: 304-293-7882
Fax: 304-293-6944
www.naftc.wvu.edu

Earn while you learn
in an apprenticeship
program.

ATHLETIC TRAINER

BECOME AN ATHLETIC TRAINER

To succeed, athletes need to be in top physical condition, and nearly all professional athletes work with top-notch coaches and athletic trainers. Athletic trainers specialize in the prevention and treatment of sports injuries.

Ordinary people looking to get in better shape are also increasingly turning to physical trainers, who usually work in gyms assisting with exercise routines and goal-setting. Both kinds of trainers sometimes also work in hospital and health care settings.

While most athletic trainers have a bachelor's degree in athletic training, certification as a physical trainer is quick and inexpensive and does not require a college degree. Two of the most highly-regarded certificates can be obtained from the American Council on Exercise (ACE, www.acefitness.org) and the National Association of Sports Medicine (NASM, www.nasm.org).

RELATED CAREERS

If the profile of an athletic trainer feels good to you, but you're not sure this is your path, you might want to consider other careers that require similar skills and interests.

These include:
- coaches and sports instructors
- licensed practical nurses
- nursing assistants
- orthotic and prosthetic specialists
- physical therapists
- physical therapy assistants
- recreational therapists
- respiratory therapists
- veterinary assistants

WILLIAM AND MARY
SPORTS MEDICINE WORKSHOP

Every year, the College of William and Mary hosts the William and Mary Sports Medicine Workshop — a summer camp for high school students interested in careers in athletic training and sports medicine. The William and Mary Sports Medicine Workshop is an intensive four-day curriculum designed to introduce high school students to the exciting field of sports medicine. At the core of the workshop is the American Red Cross Adult CPR course in which participants will learn vital life-saving skills and complete their CPR certification. Depending on their experience and skill level, participants can choose either the Basic Track or Advanced Track to enhance their knowledge in sports medicine.

The Basic Track curriculum includes taping and wrapping, injury prevention techniques, introduction to rehabilitation, emergency care skills, and basic injury recognition. The Advanced Track is designed for students who have attended a basic workshop and/or have extensive experience under the supervision of their athletic trainer at their school. The Advanced curriculum includes a visit to the cadaver anatomy lab, a seminar on sports medicine careers and choosing the right college, a trip to the pool for an introduction to aquatic therapy, and labs on advanced taping and wrapping.

Please visit the camp's website for an application, photos from the previous workshops and more information: **www.wm.edu/sportsmedicine/sportsmedcamp.htm**. The cost for 2007 was $325; there are scholarships available. The camp is offered each year in the summer.

YOUTH BUILD

BUILD A FUTURE ALONG WITH A HOUSE

If you haven't finished high school, have financial need, and want to acquire skills to support yourself, YouthBuild may be for you. **YouthBuild is a nationwide public-private partnership that teaches carpentry skills to 16 to 24 year-olds.**

There are more than 225 local YouthBuild programs throughout the United States. To find the one nearest you, **visit www.youthbuild.org**.

YouthBuild offers job training and educational opportunities to unemployed young adults who learn to build and rehabilitate affordable housing in their own communities.

Participants spend 6 to 24 months in the program, dividing their time between the construction site and the YouthBuild alternative school. Community and faith-based nonprofit organizations sponsor most programs, although some are sponsored by public agencies. Each YouthBuild program raises private and public funds to support itself.

Skills Training, College Experience

In addition to learning valuable job skills, YouthBuild students get the experience of attending a community college and can earn 30 to 40 credit hours in the year-long program.

Being part of the YouthBuild program means making progress on or obtaining a GED, going to work every weekday from 8 a.m. to 4 p.m., learning construction skills, and using those skills to build two houses.

Participants are provided with books, tuition, some tools, transportation, and a wage. Students learn to build a house, read blueprints and do estimates. In addition, an innovative approach of this project combines construction skills training with entrepreneurial and small business training.

The goal of the program is to produce graduates capable of becoming economically self-sufficient by starting microenterprises and small businesses in the home construction trades. Graduates have access to resources and support to assist them as they advance their careers, go to college, build wealth, and become role models locally and nationally.

WILLIAMSON FREE SCHOOL
OF MECHANICAL TRADES

A UNIQUE OPPORTUNITY TO LEARN A TRADE

The Williamson Free School of Mechanical Trades in Media, Pennsylvania, is the only free boarding school of its kind in the nation. In three years, students study trades and technical theory, work on realistic projects, and receive academic instruction in a highly disciplined environment.

According to the director, Edward Bailey, young men coming out of this program can expect to get jobs starting from $45,000 to $60,000 per year.

By completing the three-year program, students earn an Associate Degree in Construction Technology with an emphasis in carpentry or masonry; horticulture, landscaping, and turf management; or machine tool, power plant, or structural coatings technology.

Craftsman Diplomas are awarded in carpentry, machine trades, masonry, painting and wall covering, and power plant operations.

The educational program emphasizes the importance of moral values, industry, and quality workmanship. The goal is to foster in students attitudes that will lead to success in life and on the job, including self-discipline, integrity, and reliability.
www.williamson.edu

You know you have survival skills, but you can't see yourself starting your own business? Would you like to learn how to turn your resourcefulness into a way to start a business?

New approaches to business training are helping people who usually do not see themselves as business-minded redefine themselves and use the skills they already have.

Q: INTERESTING . . . HOW DO I FIND THIS KIND OF TRAINING?

A: First, almost every community has a Small Business Development Center led by the Small Business Administration. Most of these are connected with colleges and provide inexpensive training courses in business topics. Assistance from these centers is available to anyone interested in beginning a small business or improving or expanding an existing small business. For a list of offices, see **www.sba.gov/localresources**.

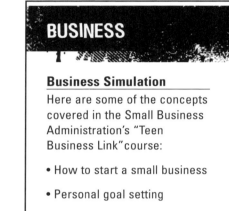

BUSINESS

Business Simulation

Here are some of the concepts covered in the Small Business Administration's "Teen Business Link" course:

• How to start a small business

• Personal goal setting

• Choosing a bank for your business

• How to get a business license

• Understanding the role of marketing

Business Simulation Course

Consider taking a free, hands-on, "learning by doing" training course called Making Cents Business Simulation.

Making Cents developed this course based on its business experience. Since 1988, this kind of training has helped 60,000 unemployed people to become self-employed.

The course takes place over a period of four or five weeks, one evening a week. In the course, you will deal with real-life problems that come up in starting and managing an imaginary business.

To learn more about Making Cents, visit **www.makingcents.com**.

Finally, check out websites with "business start-up kits" that help you think through the steps of starting a business.

One that's especially good is the **www.sba.gov/teens/** designed for young first-timers.

INTERNET RESOURCES

- **www.jamieallen.com/youthlinks.htm**

- **www.nxlevel.org** has a youth entrepreneur curriculum called "What's the Buzz on Biz"

- **studentcenter.ja.org** has tons of resources directed at high school students, including a Business Start Up kit

- **www.independentmeans.com** holds Camp $tart Up for youth in June and July

- **www.edtecinc.com** Education, Training and Enterprise Center

"Make the world a
**CLEANER &
SAFER PLACE"**

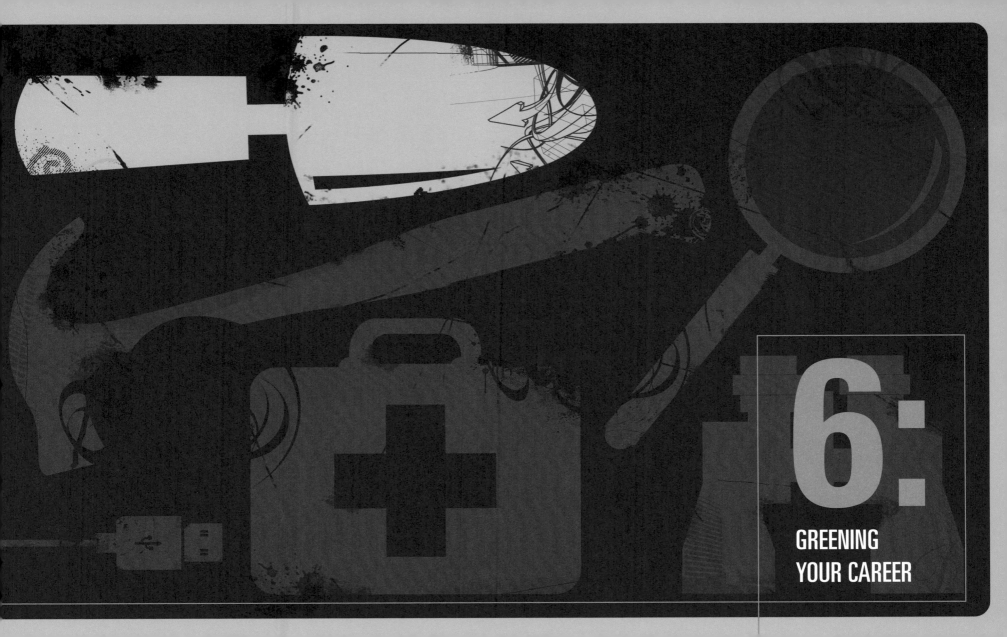

6:
GREENING
YOUR CAREER

WHAT IS A GREEN BUSINESS?

Many people prefer to work outdoors in nature. Others care about what happens to the environment and want to be part of the solution. If you fall into either of these groups, seeking out a "Green Job" may be for you.

Many, many websites list environmental internships. This is a great way to get your feet wet and find out if this is an area you'd enjoy working in. For outdoors lovers, it's a great mix of serving your country while breathing in fresh air!

WHAT'S A GREEN BUSINESS?

Green Businesses are involved in producing or selling many products that support the environment. Jobs in health food businesses, organic farming or manufacturing, and green building are available. More and more businesses are recognizing the importance of producing goods that are environmentally sustainable.

Green businesses sell all types of consumer goods and services. Thousands of green businesses are listed in the National Green Pages.
www.coopamerica.org/pubs/greenpages/

If a Green Business is something you think would be worth your time and effort to learn about, keep reading.

Sustainable business does not have a huge number of jobs yet, but check out some of the examples below and surf the Internet for more. If you see one you like, give a call and see if an intern is needed.

Green Dream Jobs

One good site for a green dream job is **www.sustainablebusiness.com/jobs**. See the next page for a few sample listings from that site:

GREEN
DREAM JOBS

Do you want to make a difference with your life, your work? Would you like to work with people who share your vision of sustainability and would welcome your thoughts about an organic lifestyle?

Terressentials

Highly motivated, environmentally-aware, and organically-minded people can join with us to help raise global organic consciousness by providing folks with healthier, organic personal care products. We are a small, rapidly growing, unique organic activist and education-based company that is making a real difference in the organic marketplace on an international basis.

Learn about our business from the ground up and grow organically with us! Participate in production: mixing/blending, bottling/packaging, labeling or shipping. Assist with customer service and education, providing face-to-face, telephone and email education and customer service.**www.terressentials.com**

Organic Farming Internship at Smokey House Center (Danby, Vermont)

Organic gardening internships provide an introduction to organic gardening techniques.

Responsibilities: Interns in the organic gardens will work independently and alongside youth crews in the everyday operation of Smokey House's diversified organic farm. Much of the work will focus on the 1.5 acre organic vegetable gardens which supply a 40-member CSA program and weekly farmer's market sales. Interns will learn about soil preparation, seeding, transplanting, weed and pest control, irrigation, greenhouse management, harvesting, and marketing as they assist in carrying out these tasks. Other work may include, but not be limited to, blueberry cultivation and harvesting, haying, animal husbandry, and Christmas tree care. Positions available from mid-May through mid-October.

Qualifications: Genuine interest in working on a small, diversified, organic farm, ability to work as part of a team, driver's license in good standing, ability to carry out hard physical labor, willingness to work in extremes of heat and sun, and cold and rain. Some background in agriculture is helpful but not necessary. Housing and a stipend are provided. Educational internships are also available.

For an application contact: Joe Przypek, Smokey House Center, 426 Danby Mountain Rd., Danby, VT 05739-9771, Ph: 802-293-5121, Email: fieldstudies@vermontel.net

NATURAL BUILDING INTERN

Natural Building Intern (Heathcote Community, Freeland, MD)

Heathcote Community in Freeland, Maryland, offers an internship in natural building and sustainable community living.

A minimum one-month commitment is required. This internship is a way to gain experience with construction and natural building techniques while exploring sustainable community living.

Interns work 40 hours a week on a new straw bale building. In exchange, they receive room and full tuition to Heathcote's summer series of workshops on natural building. They pay $150 a month for food and participate in the cooking rotation. Interns are housed in the community's 150-year-old historic grain mill and integrated into all aspects of community life, including meetings and social events.

Heathcote Community is located on 110 wooded acres in northern Baltimore County, Maryland. This community has an organic and vegetarian diet, and practices conflict resolution and consensus decision making. It has several vegetable, herb, and flower gardens; bees; hiking trails; and stream-side hammocks.

Internships are also available in gardening and homeschooling. Interested applicants complete a written application, an interview, and a community visit.

For information, call Jette at 410-357-8890 or Karen Stupski at 410-343-3478. Email: naturalbuilding@heathcote.org. Website: **www.heathcote.org**

Family helping to toss bales on a project building houses for seasonal agricultural workers in Omak, WA. Straw-bale housing is especially well-insulated and made out of renewable materials, and therefore very green. Photo courtesy of The Iron Straw Group **www.ironstraw.org**, a nonprofit that builds and promotes sustainable bale building practices.

"Green businesses operate in ways that solve, rather than cause, both environmental and social problems."
–Coop America

If you love nature and are worried about our environment, jobs and internships are available for getting valuable experience for a future career. You can find many opportunities on the Web, and several are listed here.

The Student Conservation Association (SCA)

The SCA offers a variety of volunteer and paid experiences in U.S. national parks. Crews of six to ten students (high school, college, or others) with two adult leaders build and maintain trails; construct shelters, rock walls, and bridges; restore habitat; and remove invasive species.

You might be sent deep into the backcountry, to more accessible parklands, or into well-populated communities. Crews live and work out of a base camp, sleep in tents, and share cooking and cleaning. There are also opportunities to volunteer in local programs in eight urban districts.

SCA provides housing, a living stipend, possible academic credit, AmeriCorps education awards, health and accident insurance, and travel to the project site. Partners include the National Park Service, the U.S. Forest Service, and other federal, state, and nonprofit organizations.

For a list of hundreds of current positions, go to **www.thesca.org.**

To apply, simply email your resumé, a list of positions you are interested in, availability dates, and current contact information.

Contact information:
Email: joinus@thesca.org.
Phone: 603-543-1700 for questions.

The Environmental Careers Organization (ECO)

This organization is a clearinghouse for information about environmental internship opportunities and a lot more **www.eco.org**. The opportunities are for people already in college.

At ECO's Career Center, you'll find career tips, answers to your questions, links to other sites, and brief information about environmental fields. You can read about several career paths—from water quality to forestry to education.

ECO's book, "*The Complete Guide to Environmental Careers in the 21st Century*"—which you can read right on their website—is a great source of information about environmental, conservation, and sustainability careers. Go to **www.eco.org**, click on "Publications," and then click "Read it on-line."

ECO Careers places about 700 interns each year in 35 states. On their site they answer all sorts of questions about these internships. Read their frequently asked questions for all you'll need to know about their internship program.

Orion Grassroots Network

This network is an environmental internship and career service connecting students and professionals with cutting-edge environmental and social change work. **www.oriononline.org**

Orion's Internship & Career Service advertises internships, jobs, apprenticeships, and AmeriCorps opportunities available with 800 members of their network.

These organizations do vital, place-based work in conservation, education, restoration, agriculture, and activism.

Appalachian Coal Country Watershed

The OSM/VISTA Watershed Team is a partnership between the Office of Surface Mining (OSM) and AmeriCorps VISTA (Volunteers in Service to America). The team places full-time VISTA volunteers in community watershed associations throughout Appalachian coal country, which includes 30 sites in 8 states (Pennsylvania, Maryland, Ohio, West Virginia, Virginia, Tennessee, Kentucky, Alabama). The majority of the sites are in rural communities with a history of coal mining.

Full-time interns working 12-month stints are responsible for organizing stream monitoring programs for their watersheds and researching long-term solutions to environmental problems, such as acid mine drainage. They also play a key role in educating young people in their communities about litter prevention, acid mine drainage, and other water quality issues.

They create newsletters, write press releases, talk one-on-one with members of the community to inform them of important issues, and recruit their help with various projects, such as the removal of litter from stream banks and dump site clean-ups.

Interns earn a small living allowance (approximately $750/month), health insurance, childcare (if eligible), student loan forbearance (interest paid for a year deferment by the federal government), choice of $1,200 stipend or $4,725 education award (upon successful completion of term), training, and an opportunity to make a difference.

If you can work effectively with a wide range of people, are motivated to identify needs and find resources to meet those needs, have a strong desire to help improve the quality of life for the people of Appalachia, have excellent writing and public speaking skills, and are computer literate, this may be the opportunity for you.

For full details,
www.accwt.org/volunteer.html

COLLEGE-LIKE PROGRAMS

Some colleges offer special programs for people who want to do something different.

- **Castle Rock Institute for Wilderness Adventure and the Humanities**
  North Carolina's Brevard College offers programs primarily for college students but also accepts recent high school graduates who'd like to earn humanities course credit, engage in outdoor adventure activities, and live in a small community setting. Locations include North Carolina, South Carolina, and Australia. **www.castle-rock.org**

- **The Audubon Expedition Institute, Lesley University**
  This program is one of the top five Outdoor Education programs. With "the desert Southwest, Alaska, Hawaii, and other sweet spots," for their campus, AEI students explore diverse bioregions living on buses as they pursue environmental studies. High school graduates participate in its experiential ecology programs as a post-graduation year. **www.lesley.edu/gsass/audubon**

NICHE FARMING

Farming takes many forms—from large-scale poultry production to small organic truck farming.

No matter what the scale of the farm, though, today's farmer is using new approaches and business know-how to succeed.

Many farmers are pioneering in shaping their businesses to respond to new demands for grass-fed cattle, goat meat and milk, organic fruit, vegetables, flowers, herbs, sprouts, and many other products.

Many are exploring "sustainable farming" techniques that produce healthy products and save the earth at the same time.

Numerous farms producing these specialized products are scattered throughout the country. Many can provide internship opportunities if you want to learn the business.

You don't have to grow up on a farm to become a farmer! You don't have to live in the country, either—urban agriculture is a growing phenomenon!

Find Hundreds of Organic Farm Sites Worldwide

World-Wide Opportunities on Organic Farms (WWOOF) helps individuals find organic farmers in countries around the world.

Students or others join a WWOOF organization in a particular country of interest and are then put in contact with host farms to make particular arrangements. Interns work 6 hours a day, 6 days a week. They receive no pay, but do get room and board with the host family.

Responsibilities may include sowing, making compost, gardening, planting, cutting wood, weeding, making mud-bricks, harvesting, fencing, building, typing, packing, milking, and feeding.

See listings for organic farms at **www.wwoof.org**.

Southeastern Willing Workers on Organic Farms (SEWWOOF)

SEWWOOF is a service linking organic farmers in the southeastern United States with people interested in apprenticeships in farming. Membership costs $20 and you will need to become a member to access a list of farms willing to accept workers.

It publishes the SEWWOOF Farm List, which describes each farm's operation, compensation, etc.
www.wwoofusa.org/directory.html

Contact information:
Mailing address: P.O. Box 134, Bonlee, NC 27213
Email: sewwoof@crosswinds.net

GETTING STARTED

There are many websites you can check out to get more information on internships and apprenticeships in organic and sustainable farming. The three listed below should help get you started.

- Farms offering internships or apprenticeships may be found in a registry maintained by ATTRA—National Sustainable Agriculture Information Service, an organization that provides information and resources to the U.S. agriculture community. If you are interested in on-farm internships, please check the ATTRA website: **www.attrainternships.ncat.org**.

- Organic Volunteers can provide a directory of volunteer opportunities or educational exchange opportunities in organic farming. **www.organicvolunteers.com**

- **www.backdoorjobs.com**

ORGANIC FARMING
APPRENTICE

Organic Farming Apprentice (Worden Farms, Punta Gorda, Florida)

Worden Farm raises organic vegetables, fruits, herbs, flowers, certified-transitional-organic oranges, and a small herd of grass-fed natural beef cattle. The farm is on the southern Gulf Coast of Florida, in an area of cattle ranches, orange groves, pinelands, and beaches.

Apprentices are hosted during the Florida winter vegetable season, from September through June. The minimum stay is two months. Work schedule is five and a half days per week. Preference is given to full-season applicants with professional interest in agriculture. Apprentices get hands-on education in organic crop production and marketing, through informal farm skill demonstrations. Tasks include planting, greenhouse management, transplant production, irrigation projects, crop maintenance, harvesting, and direct marketing through farmers' markets and the CSA (Community Sustainable Agriculture) farm membership program.

Optional college credit for the apprenticeship is available through an educational partnership between Worden Farm and the University of Florida. College credit can be earned at either undergraduate or graduate level. All apprentices have access to the farm's sustainable agriculture reference library.

Apprentices receive $500 per month, with a paid vacation of one day per month worked. Housing is provided on the farm in air-conditioned cabins. Apprentices have a shared kitchen and access to the produce from the farm fields for all meals. Smoking, drugs, and alcohol are not permitted.

To apply, email a letter of interest and resume, with three references. Email: office@wordenfarm.com. Web site: **www.wordenfarm.com**.

TRAINING IN SUSTAINABLE FARMING

The rich earth can be your best friend. Where else can you be your own boss, eat wholesome food, earn a good living, and heal the planet?

You can learn to run your own successful small farm in a number of different ways, from classroom learning to hands-on farming through a community organization. Below is a list of just some of the many options available.

There are college programs in sustainable farming available in nearly every state across the country. Some are complete college credit programs, but many offer community classes through statewide agricultural extension programs and community projects.

Perhaps the best all-around guide to get you started is through the Alternative Farming Systems Information Center (AFSIC) maintained by the National Agricultural Library (NAL) in Maryland.

The U.S. and international institutions and organizations in the AFSIC directory are selected based on their programs offering education, training or information in organic, alternative, or sustainable agriculture.

The following directories also may be helpful:

The Northeast Organic/Sustainable Agriculture Education Directory describes educational and training programs about organic or sustainable agricultural methods in the northeastern region of the United States.

Contact: The Northeast Organic Farming Association, Massachusetts Chapter 411 Sheldon Road Barre, MA 01005
Phone: 978-355-2853
Email: nofa@nofamass.org
www.nofamass.org/programs/ageddirectory.php

Upper Midwest Organic Resource Directory entries include contact information and descriptions of university organic or sustainable agricultural programs plus other sources that may offer educational training opportunities.

Contact: Midwest Organic and Sustainable Education Service
P.O. Box 339
Spring Valley, WI 54767
Phone: 715-772-3153.
Email: info@mosesorganic.org.
www.mosesorganic.org/umord/directory.htm

The Organic Agriculture Centre of Canada Directory lists courses, program descriptions, and contact information for institutions in Canada that offer training in organic agriculture.

Contact: Nova Scotia Agricultural College
P.O. Box 550
Truro, Nova Scotia, Canada B2N 5E3.
Dr. Ralph Martin, Director
Phone: 902-893-7256
Fax: 902-896-7095
Email: oacc@nsac.ns.ca
www.organicagcentre.ca/Courses/courses_campus_credit.html

CONTACT INFORMATION

For a good clearinghouse of information on options for obtaining training in sustainable farming, contact the Alternative Farming Systems Information Center (AFSIC). Their website lists an abundance of resources for both college-focused and community oriented training opportunities.

Alternative Farming Systems Information Center

National Agricultural Library
10301 Baltimore Avenue, Room 132
Beltsville, MD 20705-2351
Phone: 301-504-6559
Fax: 301-504-6927
Web: **afsic.nal.usda.gov**

www.nal.usda.gov/afsic/pubs/edtr/EDTR2006.shtml contains the database of educational and training opportunities in sustainable agriculture.

Additional Opportunities

There are a few nonprofit organizations that provide hands-on training in sustainable agriculture, including the Massachusetts-based Food Project. The Food Project offers fellowships for young people. Read more:

FOOD PROJECT
FELLOWSHIP

Since 1991, **The Food Project** has built a national model of engaging young people in personal and social change through sustainable agriculture. Each year, we work with more than a hundred teens and thousands of volunteers to farm on 31 acres in rural Lincoln, Massachusetts and on several lots in urban Boston. We consider our hallmark to be our focus on identifying and transforming a new generation of leaders by placing teens in unusually responsible roles, with deeply meaningful work. The Food Project creates fertile ground for new ideas about youth and adults partnering to create social change through sustainable agriculture.

Our Goal

Sustainable, local food systems that bridge race, class, age, and more to ensure food security for all.

The work of the organization depends fundamentally on the participation of young people, so The Food Project is committed to increasing the range of opportunities and scope of responsibility available to young people within the organization. The Fellowship program was designed to provide an opportunity for an alumnus to have a continuing and more substantial involvement in the organization.

Currently, a Food Project Fellowship is a full-time, one-year staff apprenticeship position. With close supervision, Fellows take on staff responsibilities in one or more areas of the organization. During their year, they design and conduct a research project.

Who Can Apply

Any young person ages 18 to 24, who is passionate about The Food Project vision and mission may apply. Typically, young people applying for this position are taking a year off from college; are postponing college for a year; or have been working.

Our mission is to grow a thoughtful and productive community of youth and adults from diverse backgrounds who work together to build a sustainable food system. We produce healthy food for residents of the city and suburbs and provide youth leadership opportunities. Most importantly, we strive to inspire and support others to create change in their own communities. For more information about this unique opportunity, see **www.thefoodproject.org** or write to info@thefoodproject.org.

TRAINING PROGRAM

If you are interested in a more formal training program, the Farm School might be what you are looking for. The Farm School Practical Farm Training Program offers a hands-on curriculum in learning how to be a farmer. More formal than usual farm apprenticeships and designed specifically for the beginning farmer, college credit may be arranged. Tuition is $10,000 and only limited financial aid is available.

Practical Farm Training Program:
Jennifer Core
The Farm School
Sentinel Elm Farm
488 Moore Hill Road
Athol, MA 01331
Phone: 978.249.2656
Email: Jennifer@farmschool.org
Web: **www.farmschool.org**

Where else can you be your own boss?

"Be the master of **YOUR EDUCATION**"

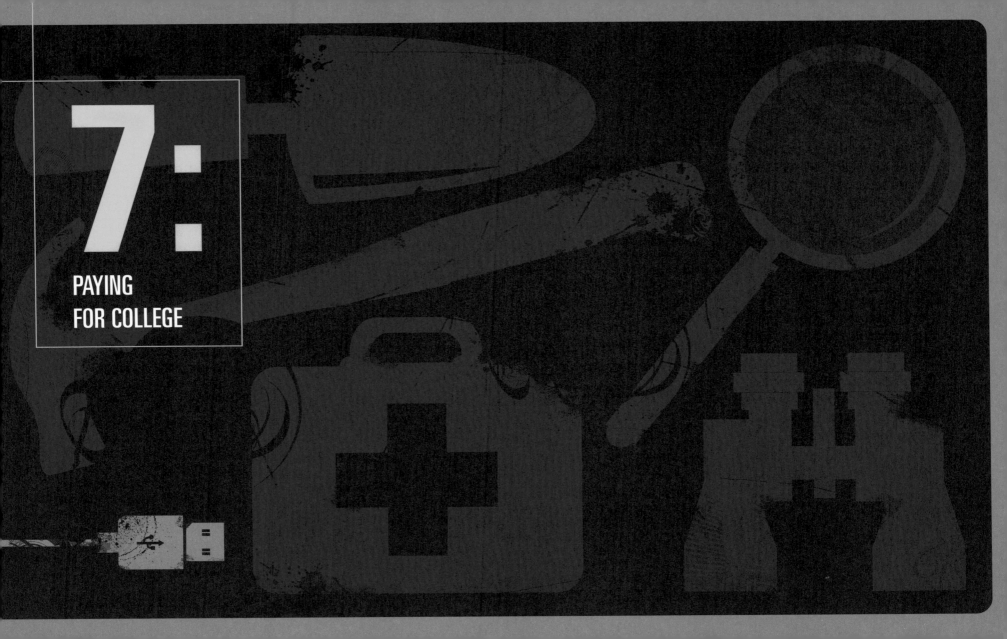

7:

PAYING
FOR COLLEGE

Being a college or university student is hard, but it's also fun and exciting. It's a time in life where you can concentrate fully on learning what you enjoy and on what will help you find a well-paid and meaningful career.

Quite a few myths are out there, however, about getting into college and paying for college.

So before you let the myths discourage you, check out this section on the real story about paying for an education.

PUBLIC AND PRIVATE COLLEGES OFFER DEGREES IN ALL AREAS OF PROFESSIONAL LIFE.

Degrees vary in time and cost, ranging from a two-year associate's degree for many skilled labor professions (e.g., nurse, mechanic) to a four-year bachelor's degree and beyond (masters and doctoral degrees).

WORRIED ABOUT THE COST? IT PAYS TO STUDY THE FINANCIAL AID SYSTEM

So take some time to figure out how financial aid works. It takes a lot of work, but the more help you can find, the better you'll enjoy and focus on your studies.

Financial aid comes in many forms—you can get loans (high and low-interest), grants, stipends, and scholarships. Loans must be paid back, but the others are free money. When you apply for financial aid, make sure to check on "strings attached."

Qualified students whose families do not earn a lot of money should not shy away from applying to private colleges that appear to be too expensive. These schools often have "need-based" aid, and if they are interested in you (combination of good grades, involvement in interesting activities, demographic status, where you live, etc.), they often will provide large grants in aid to reduce your tuition costs.

Also, remember that unemployment of a parent, single-parenthood, and major expenses such as medical bills makes your application move more readily into a "need-based" category.

If you have such situations, it may be that you are eligible for more funding than you think.

One great way to get started is to head to your local college access program. **www.collegeaccess.org** has a list of local programs. The most important person in the process will be the Financial Aid Officer at the school you apply to, so relax, find your perfect school and worry about money later.

COMMUNITY COLLEGE: A GREAT OPTION

Courtney was attending her neighborhood high school, but getting really bored. She was smart, but frustrated in school and wanting to do something really different. With her parent's help, she left high school early and enrolled in a local community college that allowed early admissions. After two years, she graduated with an Associate's degree and will be attending a four-year college this fall. Even while in school, she found time to volunteer during the day, read books she was interested in, and get all of her work for school done.

Some people find that doing two years at a community college can make their four-year degree much cheaper. It's very tricky to make sure credits transfer, but many schools have transfer agreements. It pays to investigate — if you take the right classes, you can save a bundle finishing up your junior and senior year at a four-year institution. To find a community college near you, see **www.aacc.nche.edu**

Free Application for Federal Student Aid (FAFSA)

A number of government programs can help you. The Pell Grant, the Perkins Loan, and the Stafford Loan are all sources of money from the government.

To get loans and grants from the government or from most colleges, you, with your parent(s) or guardian(s), must complete a FAFSA (Free Application for Federal Student Aid).

The FAFSA is used to determine the amount of your Expected Family Contribution (EFC) and your eligibility for federal and state financial aid (e.g., verifies your age and if you registered for the Selective Service).

Ways to File Your FAFSA Application

The FAFSA form is long and confusing so don't hesitate to ask for help from your guidance counselor or the financial aid office of any college you are applying to, or visit **www.finaid.org** for useful tips and hints.

You can get a paper FAFSA application from any school. You can also fill it out online free at **www.fafsa.ed.gov**. The online FAFSA requires moving between about 50 screens, and getting an electronic PIN number for both yourself and at least one parent or guardian. This takes time, so plan ahead.

Sometimes, private colleges also require you to fill out the CSS/Financial Aid PROFILE®.

This is a more extensive investigation of your financial resources. It is worth the effort to fill it out, however, if your dream school requires it – and many of the most elite universities do.
profileonline.collegeboard.com

Each school has different procedures and rules on financial aid, so it pays to investigate what they are. A handful of elite universities recently made headlines by waiving Expected Family Contribution for those families making under a certain income threshold of about $40,000, even though normally it would be required under the FAFSA calculations. It pays to do your homework!

Other Sources of Aid

Your school counselor or public library has good information on local sources of financial aid. For example, churches, civic groups, parents, employers, Veteran's Administration, and vocational rehabilitation services all offer financial aid.

Special Circumstances

You may find yourself ineligible for federal aid based on:

- **drug conviction:** (most drug convictions do not count and most people qualify)

- **dependency status:** (i.e., you are considered a dependent until age 24 but your parents are not supporting you financially and they won't help with the forms)

- **immigration status**

- **you are not planning on registering for Selective Service** (illegal but some people do not as an act of conscience)

- **any other reason:** (no taxes filed previous year or parents don't want to reveal their finances, for example)

If you find yourself in such a situation, contact the Financial Aid Officer at the school you wish to attend. They may know of special scholarships or school funding options you may not be aware of. If your parents will not support you or you are not in contact with them, you may also petition the school to consider you as an independent student, meaning you can get financial aid even without your parents' help.

If You Don't Have "Papers" (Immigration)

Being undocumented creates a host of problems for accessing higher education and disqualifies a student for federal financial aid. There are a limited number of private scholarships. There is a good article on options at **www.finaid.org/otheraid/undocumented.phtml.**

Special Sources of Aid for Non-Registrants

If you did not register with Selective Service when you turned 18, or are considering not registering, federal law does not allow you to enroll in federally funded job training programs, or to receive federal financial aid for college.

To help those who, for reasons of conscience, do not comply with Selective Service laws, the Center on Conscience and War (CCW) provides loans from the Fund for Education and Training (FEAT) **www.feat.centeronconscience.org**. They also provide a list of schools that will help nonregistrants financially, like Earlham College **www.earlham.edu**, plus other loan sources. The explosion in the private education loan industry has recently provided another viable option.

The Education Resources Institute

The Education Resources Institute (TERI) sponsors a TERI Supplemental Loan Program that is also open to non-registrants, but has a broader goal of helping families plan and pay for college.

Through its free college information services, it helps students and families with career decisions, selecting colleges, navigating the financial aid process, and finding resources. (A co-borrower is required.)

TERI also realizes that many people need help filling the financial aid gap. To help meet this need, TERI offers loans based on good credit, with no income limitations, for elementary and secondary, undergraduate, graduate, and continuing education studies.

Founded in 1985 as a nonprofit organization, TERI has assisted more than one million students at more than 6,800 colleges and universities worldwide.

Loan Requirements:

- Either the student or the co-borrower must be a permanent U.S. resident and must have lived in the United States for at least two years.

- No educational achievement is required.

- The co-borrower must have had a positive income for at least two years.

- Loans cover a maximum period of one calendar year.

- Applications have no deadlines, but once an application is provided, the applicant has 90 days to complete the process.

Remember, in general, you will have better loan terms with a federal loan and not a private one, so investigate carefully. On the other hand, a private loan may help you do things that are not possible with a federal loan, like study at a foreign university.

RESOURCES

To find resources for financial aid information, look at information on federal and state sources of aid at **www.finaid.org**

TERI Contact Information
The Education Resources Institute
330 Stuart Street, Suite 500
Boston, MA 02116
Ph: 800-255-TERI (8374) and a representative will respond to your message within 24 hours.
Email: custserv@teri.org
www.teri.org/